Conflict for Space

A Focus on Identity Duality

Shavkat Kasymov

Hamilton Books

An Imprint of
Rowman & Littlefield
Lanham • Boulder • New York • Toronto • Plymouth, UK

I0029510

Copyright © 2017 by Hamilton Books
4501 Forbes Boulevard, Suite 200, Lanham, Maryland 20706
Hamilton Books Acquisitions Department (301) 459-3366

Unit A, Whitacre Mews, 26-34 Stannary Street,
London SE11 4AB, United Kingdom

All rights reserved
Printed in the United States of America
British Library Cataloguing in Publication Information Available

Library of Congress Control Number: 2016957275
ISBN: 978-0-7618-6874-3 (pbk : alk. paper)—ISBN: 978-0-7618-6875-0 (electronic)

Cover image © iStock.com/wildpixel

∞™ The paper used in this publication meets the minimum requirements of American
National Standard for Information Sciences Permanence of Paper for Printed Library
Materials, ANSI/NISO Z39.48-1992.

Contents

Part 1

Introduction

Over the course of human history, there have occurred thousands of wars and all have involved a conflict between two belligerent parties. This book seeks to provide an explanation for the outbreak of conflicts and answer the question why there are always two parties to any conflict, whether a global war, a local conflict, a cross-regional confrontation, or an inter-personal conflict. While my explanation of conflict duality may not be a conclusive one given the unique nature of the approach and absence of previous studies, I will attempt to expose the cause of conflicts and wars and answer the question why are there always two parties to any conflict and war. According to my hypothesis, every society, whether an independent nation-state, a province in a country, a city, a region of the world, or even a family experiences internal tensions as a result of a confrontation, hereafter referred to as *a conflict between a conservative and a liberal identity*. In contrast to the clash of civilizations theory[1], I argue that the main conflict in the world is between a conservative and a liberal identity.

The focal point of this book is a conflict for space which occurs between two identity groups. I argue that both world wars were fought between a conservative and a liberal identity. It seems reasonable to argue that countries tend to form alliances on the basis of mutual support networks established between their ruling identity groups in an attempt to maximize their influence across space and with the ultimate goal of establishing a global order built on their collective rule. The rise to power of military dictatorships in countries of Europe in the 20th century marked the beginning of the process of alliance building among the identities that had seized power, most prominently in Italy, Germany and Japan to overcome the dominance of a different, liberal identity group. The rise to power of the ultra-nationalism, or

National Socialism in Europe signaled the rise of conservatism in its extreme form.

The nature of the populations in modern nation states tends to be dyadic, despite the fact that there exist a myriad of political parties and movements. Process of democratic elections exemplifies the struggle for dominance over space and political contestation which constantly occurs in all polities. A good example is a contestation for high public office by two major presidential candidates representing two major parties which denote two opposing fronts in any given polity. In a situation preceding a war, whether a global conflict or a civil war, various dispersed political parties, national, ethnic, and religious groups always tend to coalesce by forming two antagonistic social fronts. There does not exist any particular study explaining the nature of this phenomenon. I find an explanation to it in a perennial struggle for space between a conservative and a liberal identity. In a typical democratic polity like the United States, for centuries only two major parties vie for political power at all levels of the state system. The division of the American society along the lines of the political affiliation; i.e., Republican versus Democrat, underlies a typical dichotomy of human society. It proved to be the cause of the American Civil War, fought between the Democratic North and the Republican South, representing a liberal north and a conservative south. Contestation for space between a conservative and a liberal identity lies at the core of all conflicts that already occurred or will occur in the future.

People can side with a diverse array of political parties, but in times of utmost political and economic crises, when internal contradictions reach a critical point; various political, ethnic, religious, or national factions always unite in a process of forming two opposing fronts which always serves as a prelude to a violent conflict, whether a local conflict or a global war. All in all, the struggle for dominance and power between two antagonistic fronts representing two human identities is what underlies the essence of modern domestic politics and international affairs, whereby states strive to forge alliances on the basis of the identity linkages established between their ruling identity groups, rather than in a pursuit of materialistic goals.

LIBERAL PEACE AND CONFLICT OF IDENTITIES

According to the liberal peace articles formulated by Immanuel Kant, a liberal democratic form of government is the optimal form of governance system in nation states.[2] Kant argues that states should have a republican, liberal form of government that can guarantee legal equality and personal liberty for its citizens which is a precursor to internal peace.[3]

A civil constitution in every state shall be republican. A constitution established, first on principles of the *freedom* of the members of a society (as individuals), second on principles of the *dependence* of all upon a single common legislation (as subjects), and third on law of their *equality* (as citizens of a state) . . . . –is a republican constitution.[4]

Relevant in this context is a study done by Danilovic and Clare who focus on distinct aspects of Kantian liberal democracy, namely, constitutionalism and democratic representation, both of which are essential for the long-lasting peace in polities:

our results reinforce the need for a careful differentiation between liberal constitutionalism and democratic representation as two related but also distinct aspects of what is referred to as 'liberal democracy'.[5]

Constitutionalism (i.e., the respect of personal liberties and the rule of law) is essential for sustaining the domestic peace since democratic representation cannot provide a social environment conducive to peace in a situation when antagonistic identity groups constantly vie for political power and dominance over space within polities. The principle of democratic representation endows the majority identity groups in power with a moral and political legitimacy for political and social predominance over the minority group. Thus, countries can have a strong democratic foundation but weak constitutionalism and still experience civil strife as outcome of the absence of checks on state leadership representing a majority identity group by the minority identity group as well as the policies of regimes that can be repressive towards them owing to the fact that all political systems are based on the rule of the majorities. Rather than ideology, pursuit of common interests, or political goals, it is the identity linkages among individuals that play a central role in a community formation and, thereby, the major processes underlying state-building, nation-building, and international affairs. Moreover, it is the identity linkages that unite people in a common effort to advance and bring to fruition certain political and ideological concepts, such as what the process of a revolution, nationalism, or electoral support represents. It is thus erroneous to view conflict strictly as outcome of certain factors such as nationalism, inequality, poverty, repressions, as those are merely manifestations of a struggle for space between the antagonistic identity groups.

Ideally, the purpose of constitutionalism is to provide universal equality before the law. Democracy is associated with the rule of law and a guaranteed protection of personal liberties by the state but having a democratic system does not guarantee a social order based on the equality of its citizens before the law since constitutionalism often serves as a vehicle for the contending identity groups to promote their inherent interests related to propagation across space.[6] In this light, it is important to distinguish democracy from constitutionalism which presupposes legal equality and personal dignity guaranteed by the state since a state system becomes an instrument of political domination in the hands of the majority identity group aimed at the minority group. Thus, on the one hand, democracy and constitutionalism can be entwined and mutually reinforcing political concepts since each regime and the identity group behind it constructs laws in accordance with its own perceptions of individual liberty, common good, and the ideal social order. Correspondingly, identities in power create laws that are geared to accommodate their particularistic interests, first and foremost. On the other hand, democracy and constitutionalism can be viewed as greatly distanced political concepts, though formally they may seem to have a direct correlation and linkage as in certain situations law can easily become an instrument of political manipulation in the hands of the identity group in power to buttress its propagation policy through the repression of a minority group. That is to say, *d e facto* many formal laws established to comply with international conventions and various framework agreements are being overridden by informal laws and practices prevalent within the identity groups in power aimed at the maximization of dominance and expulsion of an alien identity group.

Specifically, some of the universal human rights enshrined in a constitution of any nation state such as a right to life, education, adequate healthcare, employment, and residence are being routinely infringed through practices of concealed discrimination by the dominant identity group aimed at expulsion and elimination of an alien identity group on the grounds of unsuitability in any particular locale and institution. This makes those rights formally universal, whereas *de facto* they are subjected to state- and local-level interpretations and adaptation. It is, therefore, appropriate to question the universality of such international conventions given the fact that there exist multiple local definitions of human rights primarily attached to members of the dominant identity group, with many individuals of non-aligned identity group being *de facto* treated in ways that directly infringe the universality principle of human rights. Individuals representing a minority group are thus unable to find a suitable locale and are trapped in a situation of being an alien identity group whose rights are being violated on a regular basis by the majority identity group and whose social status suits that of being "second-class citizens", especially when it comes to the distribution of public posts, privileges, positions in a social hierarchy, financial assets, and properties among the general population and the resulting social stratification along the lines of the identity affiliation. In a similar fashion, a disabled individual is naturally placed at a disadvantage, or being an alien, among people lacking any kind of impairment.[7]

Process of migration is illustrative of the policies of the majority identity groups in nation states aimed at expulsion of an alien identity group which, in turn, seeks to coalesce with the overlapping identity group in order to constitute a majority in other locales through the process of migration. I argue that world society is divided into two antagonistic identity groups, a conservative and a liberal identity owing to a dichotomous nature of human conflict and dyadic political competition. That is to say, all conflicts are perennially fought between two belligerent fronts representing various social strata, national, ethnic and religious groups. Political contestation in human societies similarly takes place between two major political fronts, generally represented by two major candidates for high public office. In other words, all human societies are democratic in so far as they ruled by the leadership which embodies the will of the majority of the population or groups that possess the highest degree of potential in political, economic, and military terms but democracy is a highly ambiguous term and concept since it merely endows the majority identity groups with power to legitimately dominate over other groups which constitute the minorities within polities. However, groups in power can also be the minority groups, for they can only achieve a leadership position with the support of the overlapping identity group. Democracies can have different forms but the content is in fact identical in every geo-political setting, namely, all polities are being ruled by the leadership which is the embodiment of the will of the majority of the population or its most potent identity groups.

Individuals, representing distinct identity groups always tend to take advantage of the identity bonds with the overlapping identity group situated in other locales. These transnational identity bonds are being continuously expanded and reinforced through migration and political contestation with the opposing identity group. The main objective behind this rivalry is the expansion of the identity presence across space through the maximization of the homogeneity and expulsion of an alien identity group. Practices of concealed discrimination constitute the core of the expulsion policy. They include, but are not limited, to denying the most basic opportunities for social integration and personal realization such as education, employment, lodging, and social services for reasons undisclosed. However, the key motive behind such practices of community rejection lies in an innate policy of regionally-defined identity groups to buttress the internal homogeneity and territorial dominance over the adversary group.

Liberalism and democracy can also be viewed as intimately entwined philosophical categories owing to the fact that all societies are democratic and liberal in so far as the vast majority of countries tend to be ruled by regimes that represent the majority of the population or most potent identity groups, yet espouse unique notions of human liberty and, correspondingly, social order. It is these deviations in perceptions and expressions of freedom that lead to a contestation for space and conflicts between identity groups within and between polities.

Thus, it is misleading to present the process of a revolution or coup as loss of trust and allegiance in the regime since ruling regimes are always sustained through the unwavering support of the overlapping identity group within and beyond the territorial confines of nation states which provides them with support in a pursuit of a territorial dominance through the monopolization of administrative and executive functions in the state system and whose interests they constantly tend to represent while in power. Their success at remaining in power depends on their ability to attract the support of the overlapping identity group from other locales by way of migration and the maximization of dominance.[8] By doing this, identity groups in power secure their dominance over space through population preponderance and a policy of exclusion of an alien identity group. For example, with the advent of globalization, the role of ethnic Diasporas in the domestic politics and economy has increased dramatically thereby rendering states more inter-dependent since Diasporas tend to sustain close connection with the countries of origin. Ethnic Diasporas also reflect a convergence of underlying identity groups.

The root cause of conflict is in that distinct identities have divergent and even contradictory understandings and conceptions of liberty which sheds light on why various groups tend to collide by way of political or military confrontations for they all fight to protect their innate perceptions of freedom and liberal democracy. Since democracies can be different, so can be liberty. According to my explanation of conflict duality, different identity groups have dissimilar interpretations of liberty from which derive their incongruent ways of envisioning and building democracy. Liberty is not an absolute political category, but a relativistic notion. Different identity groups possess unique conceptions of democracy according to their inherent perceptions of individual freedom and common space. This highlights the differences in interpretations and expressions of democracy. Furthermore, it is erroneous to describe certain polities as autocracies, which is, in itself a highly biased term since it is always associated with the belligerent politics of a confront-ing identity group. Namely, Asian democracy can be different from western democracy, but having its own intrinsic cultural and social qualities does not disqualify various Asian or Eurasian societies from being democratic, or those ruled by the people or being different from western democracies.

Democracy and constitutionalism can also be conceptually segregated since different regimes that come to power construct laws that benefit pri-marily their respective identity group rather than the adversary group given the dyadic nature of political competition, to which I refer as a contestation for space between the antagonistic identity groups. That is to say, groups in power and the identities behind them benefit most, even in a modern consti-tutional state since their constructed mode of constitutionalism protects their inherent and indigenous vision of human liberty, social order and thereby democracy. Ideally, constitutionalism and separation of powers provide a framework for equitable distribution of powers among rival identity groups within the state system. Constitutionalism equalizes members of the two divergent fronts before the law under the concept of citizenship. Given the fact that the basic principles of democracy, such as the separation powers and checks and balances of political powers, provide a rational-legal foundation for the distribution of powers among the competing groups within a state system; presidential power can be concentrated in the hands of only one identity group while the ability of the legislative branch to leverage the policies of the executive branch underscores a power sharing arrangement among the distinctive identity groups in a constitutional democracy. However, that can have different connotations given the variation in the expression of identities.

Specifically, parliaments of all countries consist of a wide variety of parties of diverse political and ideological orientations which strive to represent the populace in its entirety. Their goal is to formulate a common position on various issues of importance, from domestic to international, and to communicate it to the president, through a procedure of passing and adopting laws. However, in many cases parliaments merely serve as instruments of political and social-cultural dominance of the identity group in power and the policies it advances on the domestic and global level given the prevalence of so called "power parties" in the legislative bodies which form a majority in a parliament. That way, groups in power can formulate and adopt laws without hindrances from the opposition whose ability to wield power in a legislative process is significantly hampered. So, as a way to monopolize the political process, parliaments are being dominated by the party of the ruling identity group and its various satellites. Furthermore, the policies they seek to promote are primarily advantageous to the majority identity group in spite of the existence and prominence of the social equality concept enshrined in a constitution. Thus, the role of parliaments as an independent branch of power and legislative body is significantly undermined as a result of an innate policy of identity groups in power aimed at the monopolization of political and economic space and exclusion of an alien identity group. It is important to mention that it has been a general practice to hold parliamentary elections prior to presidential elections and the party that normally wins the majority of seats normally has candidate for the presidential post win the election. Rather than serving as a counterweight to the presidential power, parliaments can be viewed as instruments of political domination in the hands of the executive power. The same holds true for the judiciary as an independent branch of power whose purpose is to ensure equality under law. Furthermore, rather than elected, in many cases the Supreme Court and Constitutional Court judges get nominated by the presidents and their independence from the executive branch thus becomes only nominal. This holds true for countries like the United States where the Supreme Court justices get appointed "by the president and with the advice and consent of the Senate"[9]. A question of whether the Supreme Court judges should be appointed or elected is one of the central in judicial politics nowadays.

The principle of the balance of political powers is thus violated while the checks on the executive power are being seriously constrained in so far as parliaments get dominated by pro-government parties while the Supreme Court judges get appointed by the presidential decrees. Opposition parties are placed at a disadvantage in both the legislative and electoral processes relative to the ruling political parties owing to a disproportionate access to administrative and financial assets afforded to them by the affiliated political leadership. In a similar vein, rather than objective, justice becomes subjective as the judiciary becomes subordinate to the presidential power whose decisions come to serve the interests of the ruling regime thereby deteriorating the core aspects of justice, namely, the impartiality and objectivity. Ideally, constitutionalism and liberal democracy provide the basis for the contending identity groups to unite under a common goal of consolidating and expanding the nation-hood and statehood. However, since liberty is highly relativistic, identity groups often come into conflict in the framework of state ideology, particularly with respect to how to conceptualize and materialize their unique perceptions of freedom and democracy.

It is important to account for the fact that populations in modern nation-states always tend to be highly fractured. Particularly, they always tend to be divided along the lines of the political, regional, religious affiliation, and ethnic background, e.g. democratic vs. republican, socialist vs. democrat, representing various regions, whereby federalism proves to be the optimal form of governance system for maintaining a territorial integrity, social cohesion, and internal peace. Ultimately, it is the majority social groups that form the governments through the basic democratic principles such as popular vote and democratic representation. The principles of the separation of powers into the executive, the legislative and the judicial branches and checks and balances of political powers underscore a situation of the division of powers among distinct identity groups in a polity. In reality, however, identity groups always aspire to dominate all branches of power and promote policies that are principally self-centered even in the so called liberal democracies. That raises questions not only about the distinctions made in the western political discourse between liberal democracies and other forms of rule, but also about the viability of democracy as a political concept on which to rely in nation- and state-building since it merely endows the majority identity groups with power and legitimacy to dominate.

For instance, according to political philosopher John Locke,

> And thus every man, by consenting with others to make one body politic under one government, puts himself under an obligation, to every one of that society, to submit to the determination of the majority, and to be concluded by it; or else this original compact, whereby he with others incorporates into one society, would signify nothing, and be no compact, if he be left free, and under no other ties than he was in before in the state of nature. For what appearance would there be of any compact? What new engagement if he were no farther tied by any decrees of the society, than he himself thought fit, and did actually consent to? This would be still as great a liberty, as he himself had before his compact, or any one else in the state of nature hath, who may submit himself, and consent to any acts of it if he thinks fit. [10]

He further states that,

> For if the consent of the majority shall not, in reason, be received as the act of the whole, and conclude every individual; nothing but the consent of every individual can make any thing to be the act of the whole: but such a consent is next to impossible ever to be had, if we consider the infirmities of health, and avocations of business, which in a number, though much less than that of a common-wealth, will necessarily keep many away from the public assembly. [11]

More important, however, is the fact that majorities in societies tend to coalesce owing to common identity linkages rather than certain overarching political ideas much of which derive from a shared inherent vision of personal liberty and social order. In other words, it is the identity bonds that drive the processes behind the community formation, nationalism, and nation building since majorities come to power according to the most basic principle of democratic representation and materialize their respective visions for the ideal community order whereby there occurs juxtaposition with a rival identity group which envisions a distinctive interpretation of freedom and social organization. Process of political contestation between two rival identity groups within polities occurs for millennia and a democratic framework of governance provides the groundwork for the dominion of the majority identity group.

> Whosoever therefore out of a state of nature unite into a community, must be understood to give up all their power, necessary to the ends for which they unite into society, to the majority of the community, unless they expressly agreed in any number greater than the majority. [12]

The Kantian concept of a liberal peace or democratic liberalism cannot preclude a conflict in a situation of intense power struggle and highly entrenched contentions between two antagonistic social fronts which underlies the essence of all political processes at all levels of the political system, from local to national and international absent there is an impartial constitutionalism which ensures individual freedom and protection by the state. However, the state system can likewise become a vehicle for political and socio-cultural domination of the identity group in power that can transform the state system from an instrument of public protection into a system of repression and political persecution aimed at the minority group. Human populations by their nature tend to be dyadic. This has proven to be true for all the socio-political formations of human making, from empires to states and provinces to cities. They are all caught in a quagmire of the internal power struggle between two antagonistic social fronts, which I named a conservative and a liberal identity.

It is misleading to place the state at the primary level of analysis as advocated by neorealists and neoliberal institutionalists given the existence of the international power struggle between the two identity groups and the links they strive to sustain and promote which transcend the confines of modern nation states. The existence of the identity bonds undercuts not only the primacy of the nation state concept but also the significance of transnational regimes in a conventional sense since state regimes and regional alliances are created only among countries whose ruling regimes are closely aligned in terms of the identity background. Otherwise, unaligned states are normally not being acceded to such alliances and treaties dominated by a certain identity group even though it might be obvious to parties that cooperation for common good is a rational alternative to belligerent politics. In addition, there are multiple examples of alliances encompassing distinct identity groups such as regional economic partnership alliances that can only be characterized as functional *de jure*, whereas *de facto* their significance is minimal due to the prevalence of sectarian politics and narrow-interest policies aimed to benefit a dominating group. Since its establishment in 1946, the effectiveness of the UN Security Council has been significantly diminished owing to contradictory positions of Russia and China on one side and countries of western bloc, on the other. Thus, there is oftentimes a high degree of variation between the actual performance of such partnerships and their stated, or, *de jure*, commitments, since some of their members are only being nominally represented with marginal potential to influence the decision making process much of which is driven by the identity alignment.

Transnational identity bonds continue to have the most salient effect on a process of domestic power struggle and thereby international relations, which underlies the overarching objective of the identity groups aimed at a territorial expansion through the dominance. In particular, I stress the significance of these bonds in international politics. Groups that seek power do so in order to maximize their dominance across space within and beyond the confines of modern nation states. The ability of the two identity groups to exert power and influence determines their success or failure in the propagation of power and presence and ultimately in a process of a power struggle with the contending group.

Liberalism highlights the importance of transnational regimes and institutions in providing the impetus for cooperation among states. International regimes come into being as result of demand for cooperation that exists among countries since they are by their nature not atomic and discrete, but highly inter-connected. States tend to act in pursuit of self-interest which is, in turn, related to an inherent policy of the identity groups aimed at the proliferation across space through the process of homogenization and absorption of the overlapping identity group, which underlies the essence of domestic and international power struggle. Modern research in large part dismisses the importance of those processes.

Furthermore, much emphasis needs to be made on a pattern of shifting identity groups in power which produce corresponding shifts of alliances among states. Different groups in power tend to forge alliances only with states whose power elites belong to an overlapping identity group. In other words, states and political power, on which both realists and neoliberals rely so extensively, merely serve as a vehicle for various identity groups to advance their inherent policies related to the territorial dominance. The struggle for power between the antagonistic identity groups is what constitutes the essence of domestic political and social processes. The notion of state failure, namely, when states fail to properly integrate themselves in a global system of liberal, democratic and market-oriented states is ambiguous in that it occurs when exclusively anti-western regimes capture the levers of state power through an armed struggle and fail to assimilate in the world system dominated by any one identity group.

> weak countries are unable to take advantage of the global economy not just because of the lack of resources, but also because they lack strong, capable institutions. [13]

Furthermore, state failure is often associated with the inability by states to properly integrate themselves in a global economy as a result of non-alignment of identity groups and the leaderships in various countries. For instance, Russia has had strained relations with the west and the global economy as exemplified by a thorny path towards the accession into the World Trade Organization, especially during the presidency of Vladimir Putin. [14]

Realists explain the occurrence of wars between nation states in light of the perceptions of threat prevalent among them which results in both their defensive and offensive behavior. More than ever, today, countries strive to consolidate their military might, both real and fictitious in order to deter any possible attacks and reinforce their political standing relative to other actors by spending a significant share of state income on increasing their offensive and defensive potential. By doing this, states seek to, first and foremost, amplify a perception of threat in the eyes of an opponent actor or groups thereof and to deter any possible attacks from them. Yet, what is missing in that context is that state behavior with respect to defense and interaction with other states always tends to be inconsistent throughout the course of history and subject to an important dependent variable - that is, whether the leaderships in countries and their constituencies are properly aligned. Scholars of political realism such as Morgenthau would explain this in the context of human nature and the complexities of human relations. Realists argue that its individuals in power, how they act and build relations that determine the course of international politics. More importantly, however, much depends on whether or not high political leaderships and their constituencies in various countries are properly aligned in terms of their respective identity groups, for countries always tend to have intermittent periods of cooperation, absence thereof, or hostility in the bilateral relations. In a similar fashion, it's erroneous to view the international system as anarchical since international relations are built on a process of contestation for space which constantly occurs between two antagonistic identity fronts, namely, a conservative and a liberal identity group. Thus, international relations can often follow quite a predictable pattern whereby relations among states are being built according to their mutual interest in cooperation and political affinity, much of which derives from the identity alignment and an overlapping goal of expanding the dominance over space *vis-à-vis* the adversary identity group.

IDENTITY DUALITY IN A HISTORICAL PERSPECTIVE

There are a number of prominent examples that shed light on these processes. For instance, the main objective behind the establishment of the ultra-nationalist regimes in Europe in the 20th century and their highly aggressive and expansionist ideologies was to counter the dominance of a distinct identity group, represented by the Marxist and Communist movements. Russia was, however, their main threat which was the main source of socialism propagated by a distinctive identity group whose elimination was of foremost importance to the Nazi regime. As soon as the Second World War ended with the surrender of the Axis powers, a pro-liberal identity group consolidated its rule from West Germany to Japan, Italy and other former Axis powers, with the aim of advancing global hegemony. After the Second World War ended, Japan was transformed from a primary foe into one of the closest allies of the United States through the shift of the ruling identity groups.

The importance of the identity duality and the shifting balance of powers among the identity groups is all the more important given the fact that Italy and Japan were part of the Allied forces alongside the United States, Great

Britain, France, Russia and other nations during the First World War. Another noteworthy example is a Spanish Civil War (1936-39) whose belligerent fronts were supported by major foreign powers, including Italy, the Nazi Germany, and the Soviet Union. Soon after the war ended, the nationalist movement led by General Francisco Franco, remained in power for a long period of time owing to the support he received from major western powers in the aftermath of the Second World War due to their geo-strategic considerations in light of the Cold War with the Soviet Union, and in spite of the fact that Franco was supported by the Nazi Germany and the Fascist Italy during the war. That is to say, throughout the history of US-Russian relations, periods of outright political, diplomatic and military rivalry, especially in the early Soviet era, were succeeded by the periods of cooperation and consolidation of the identity bonds among the leaderships of the nations, also known as the *Detente*.[15] In particular, the Khrushchev era reforms spearheaded under the leadership of the then-Soviet leader Nikita Khrushchev, more commonly known as the Khrushchev thaw, were centered on a massive de-Stalinization campaign whose ultimate goal was the elimination of policies, traditions, and institutions established during the reign of his predecessor, Joseph Stalin.

This period also witnessed a drastic and an unprecedented improvement of the relations between the West and the Soviet Union, during which time the countries' leaders made several official state visits. In particular, Joseph Stalin never undertook a state visit to any major western power, not to mention the Soviet-occupied East Germany when he attended the Potsdam Conference in 1945, while his successors in the Soviet Union and the United States made numerous official state visits thereafter.

In the wake of the Bolshevik Revolution in Russia in 1917, a massive campaign of reprisals in the form of executions, arrests, confiscations, and deportations was launched by the new Soviet political elite. These reprisals were primarily driven by the identity that had just seized power as a result of the revolution and were targeted against those representing an adversary identity group, which, in turn, reflected various societal strata at whose elimination the revolution was initially aimed. Those who were not affected by the numerous waves of reprisals were subjected to structural forms of discrimination and social exclusion thereafter. The ultimate goal of structural discrimination was to eliminate the threat emanated by an alien identity group and to minimize its chance of survival within the confines of the territories over which they had gained control. A second wave of reprisals commonly known as the Great Purge was initiated under the leadership of Joseph Stalin in 1937 against the so called "enemies of the people" extending both within and beyond the state apparatus. In particular, the cleansing campaign within governance institutions led to arrests and executions of some hundreds of thousands of people.

A slightly different scenario unfolded in Germany closer to the end of the Weimer Republic, which cut short of a civil war between the supporters of the monarchy, the socialists and nationalists. However, after the Nazi regime came to power in 1933, a massive emigration wave set out as a result of which thousands of those unaligned with the new government fled to other countries in order to avoid persecution, which is quite a typical scenario at a time when a reactionary leadership representing a certain identity group comes to power either through election or coup.

Notably, another and more recent illustration is the dissolution of the Soviet Union in 1991, as a result of which members of the dominant identity suddenly were rejected by the new identity group that had just seized power led by Boris Yeltsin who would then become the first President of Russia. Scores of new apparatchiks flooded the state system driving out those who were at the helm of the Soviet system as it came to a close. The shifting identities phenomenon is common to all countries and it illustrates the fractured nature of societies.

Contestation between a conservative and a liberal identity is what underlies the essence of both the domestic and global politics. A situation when one identity group takes power after another as a result of a revolution or a coup is a very common phenomenon which manifests the shifting identities. A striking manifestation of shifting identity groups is a process of redistribution of public posts, financial assets, material resources, and properties from one group to another following a change of key political leadership, such as a country president because of issues of allegiance dictated by the identity alignments.

The Cold War is an example of a contestation for space which the United States and the Soviet Union entered into in efforts to promote their respective identities. Through proxy wars and competition in space and technology, they sought to win leverage over space. During the Cold War, the United States and the Soviet Union sought to expand their influence through proxy, or civil wars. The wars, fought between the national liberationist movements and the governments of countries of Central America, Eastern Europe, Central Asia, Horn of Africa, and Southern Africa, witnessed the greatest share of external involvement by third parties, particularly, the superpowers. While the latter were supported by the United States, rebel movements were extensively backed by the Soviet government. However, what made different parties representing various social, economic, and ethnic groups, side with either of the two superpowers? According to my theory, it is their shared identities that united them. The Soviet Union was the centre of political conservatism, while the United Stated was the epicenter of liberalism.

Surprisingly, however, the US and the Soviet Union have never confronted each other openly as major belligerents in any war or even local conflict whatsoever. Rather, it is their rivalry that sustains peace in the world today. It is these two nations which constitute the modern bipolar world order, which still revolves around a contestation for space between a conservative and a liberal identity. They confront as well as supplement each other. Today, the meaning of world politics is hidden behind a thick cloud of the identity politics - a process, whereby minor countries tend to side with major centers of world conservatism and liberalism, namely, Russia and countries of the West. The recent allied invasions in Yugoslavia, Afghanistan and Iraq can be viewed as attempts by the West to bring about a shift of the identities at the helm of the state in line with a liberal identity group, for Russia and China, as modern centers of world conservatism have always voted against US proposals calling for a military intervention in foreign countries within the framework of the UN.

I argue that these shifting alliances are due to the conflicts of identities, namely a Conservative identity, in great part represented by Russia and China, and a liberal identity, represented by major western powers such as the United States, Great Britain, Germany, France, Italy, and Japan. Of course, this by no means implies that these nations are spared of internal tensions. An additional example which highlights the shifting identity alliances is the Russian Civil War (1917-1922) fought between the supporters of the Soviet state and the White Army, the proponents of the royal state. The latter was supported by major western powers, including France and Great Britain.

While Germany was the primary opponent of the United States in both world wars, it has been transformed into one of its strongest allies as soon as the Second World War came to a close. Other notable examples of shifting identities and fragmented societies are the Vichy France, the Korean peninsula divided into two parts, the secession of Taiwan from continental China, and the war in Vietnam fought between the communist North and South Vietnam supported by the United States and other western nations.

Cuba was a close ally of the United States before the revolution took place in 1953 led by Fidel Castro, which replaced the pro-American government of Fulgencio Batista. After the revolution, Cuba became a close political and economic partner of the Soviet Union and a political foe of the US. Iran was a close US ally during the reign of Shah Mohammad Reza Pahlavi until he was deposed during the Islamic revolution in 1979, turning the country into a major source of anti-Westernism in the region.

Soviet-Egyptian relations experienced a drastic change from the period of the presidency of Nasser which could be characterized as being cooperative but have deteriorated thereafter after President Sadat succeeded him in power owing to the latter's policies favorable to the relations with the West and, specifically, Israel. The *Intifah*, or the opening of the Egyptian economy, is one of the most prominent aspects of Sadat's policies aimed at improving the relations with the West.[16]

The Velvet Revolution of 1968 and the invasion by the Warsaw pact of Czechoslovakia exemplify how swiftly a country can shift allegiances as a result of the internal power struggle between the two identity groups. A pro-communist regime was taken over by pro-western activists whose aim was to undermine the influence of a conservative pro-communist identity group supported by the Soviet Union. More to the point, the creation of the Warsaw pact under the banner of fighting western imperialism with the inclusion of such countries as Bulgaria, Hungary, and Romania following their fervent support of the Nazi Germany and a struggle in the Second World War against the Soviet Union also shed light on how swiftly nations can change a political course in the wake of internal power struggle and the shifting identity groups at the helm of the state.

Regionally-defined identity groups compete for political power and economic resources within nation-states. This rivalry is a focal point of state politics and international affairs. In the international affairs realm, identity groups create new bonds and expand old ones with overlapping identities for increasing the political and economic returns of cooperation, which underpins the identities' inherent policy of proliferation. It forms the basis of alliance building policies among states whose identity groups in power are closely aligned. The countries of a conservative camp have formed an organization titled The Shanghai Organization for Security (SCO) to formally advance common interests and to demonstrate to a rival identity their alignment. The goal behind the creation of the North Atlantic Treaty Organization (NATO) in 1949 by the United States and countries of Western Europe was to safeguard a liberal identity. The Warsaw pact was created in 1955 by the Soviet Union and its allies as a counterweight to NATO. Founded in 1920 by leading western nations, excluding Germany, following the First World War to guarantee collective security, protection, and commitment to shared interests, the League of Nations was, similarly, the embodiment of aligning identities, for Germany joined in 1926 only to withdraw in 1933 with the rise to power of the Nazi party.

After a change of the government, a new governance apparatus is assembled by the new leadership comprising new cabinet members and administrations whose allegiance to the new leadership is of foremost importance, along with their expertise and aptitude. Allegiance, however, is most often dictated by the identity alignment, which explains why relatives and family members of power elite are often the ones to fill in the leadership positions in the government and affiliated institutions. Many institutions of power in countries around the world are dominated by groups of people united by the identity bonds. There is a clear delineation along the lines of the identity duality in the patterns of political appointment to the state system and the economy with groups united by a shared identity occupying key segments in a society and various identity groups filling separate economic strata, which forms the basis of social stratification.

Oftentimes, process of social cohesion is superficial and the societies are always struggling with internal contradictions. The confrontation between a conservative East and a liberal West, the Orthodox and the Catholic Church, the Shi'a and Sunni Muslims across the world are some of the most notable manifestations of a struggle between a conservative and a liberal identity. As world wars, past conquests by global powers of foreign lands, the selective enslavement, expulsion, and extermination of certain groups of the indigenous population by colonists, and modern civil wars occur as a result of a contestation for space between the two identity groups. Mass deportations and mass killing of populations are the manifestations of a struggle between the identity groups for power and dominance over space.

It is important to highlight another example which manifests a sudden shift in state and social thinking. According to Burgess, post-Soviet Russia, especially during the reign of president Putin, experienced a sudden resurgence of the orthodoxy and conservatism.

> The number of Orthodox churches in Moscow alone rose from 40 to 872. Moreover, the percentage of Russians identifying themselves as Orthodox increased from 20 per cent to perhaps as much as 80 per cent. The massive persecution of the church under communism has been followed by what seems to many Orthodox a miracle of rebirth. [17]

While some observers have noted that with the resurgence of the orthodoxy and conservatism in Russia there has occurred a synthesis of the church and the state, a return to the so called ancient conception of a "symphony" between the state and the church, it is with the arrival of new political leadership infused with the ideas of conservatism and orthodoxy that such a spiritual revival came about, which contrasts to the period of the first Russian president Boris Yeltsin.

> For many Russians, to be Russian is to be Orthodox. Nineteenth-century Slavophile ideas are still influential, casting Catholicism and Protestantism as Western imports that have belonged historically to invaders from abroad (such as Catholic Poles or Protestant Swedes and Germans). Many Russians are suspicious of Western pluralism and the notion that the individual can construct an identity, including a religious identity. Russians assume that individuals inherit a historical identity from the ethnos to which they belong. [18]

Needless to say, over the past 20 years, Russia has experienced a drastic transformation of its state policy from state atheism during the Soviet era, to a pro-western liberalism and a policy of religious and political freedom during the presidency of Boris Yeltsin and to orthodox conservatism and statism during the reign of Vladimir Putin. What makes a country as big and influential as Russia change the essence of its state policies so drastically in regards to religion and freedom of expression? Why soviet Russians so widely supported the state policy of atheism but after a change of the political leadership, the majority of ethnic Russians suddenly framed their national identity in terms of its strong connection to Orthodox Christianity? Was religious freedom so strongly suppressed in the Soviet Union as to make the Russian *ethnie* refute its centuries–old affinity to Christianity? Process of shifting identities can provide some explanation as to why such drastic changes in social thinking take place.

A CONSERVATIVE AND A LIBERAL DEMOCRACY

According to the democratic peace theory, democratic polities do not go to war with each other but can go to war with non-democratic states. What is difficult to account for how one country can be considered democratic while another autocratic? Why countries like Russia, China, or North Korea do not fall under the category of a liberal and democratic country? How can a governance system in one country be deemed as democratic while in another country as a dictatorial? For a country run by a single state party with nearly absolute support of the national population can hardly be regarded as non-democratic or illiberal. That is to say, according to the perceptions of freedom among the majority of Chinese, Russian, or North Korean populations, they can hardly be considered oppressed or unhappy with the regime. That is true for such countries as China, Russia, and others of the so called "non-democratic camp". I find an explanation to this paradox in the fact that different identity groups tend to provide unique interpretations of democracy and liberty, for countries of one group, which I call a liberal identity, tend to interpret democracy primarily in light of what is considered to be conventional notions of democratic rule, separation of powers, the triumph of personal liberties and Kantian liberal peace articles, whereas another group, to which I refer as a conservative identity group, views democracy and liberty in light of the national unity and collective trust in a national leadership that can guarantee them collective and personal freedom. Such countries champion conservative ideals rooted in the centuries' old orthodoxy, such as Buddhism and Orthodox Christianity. Countries of a liberal camp tend to view countries of a conservative camp as an antipode conglomerate of nation states. That is to say, only moderate or below moderate levels of cooperation exist between countries of the two blocs, in comparison to high levels of mutual support and integration that exist within these blocs of states.

Democratic peace theory posits that democratic polities are reluctant to engage in armed combat with other democratic states.[19]

Advocates of the democratic peace have claimed that over time, country by democratizing country, a peace would spread to cover the entire world, building one world order – democratic, free, prosperous, and peaceful.[20]

The problem with the democratic peace theory is that by democratizing a country by way of a foreign invasion, which is, in itself an ambiguous task, one cannot guarantee absolute loyalty of a country's indigenous population given the fact that some groups always tend to support such external involvement while others resist it owing to a dyadic nature of populations. Furthermore, the power struggle in nation states is always accompanied by the external involvement by countries whose constituent identity groups seek to expand their sphere of dominance by having overlapping regimes in foreign countries. This explains the active involvement of major powers such as the United States and Russia during the electoral processes and their conflicting positions when it comes to supporting particular parties, groups, and candidates for high public office.

In the course of a power struggle, various political and ethnic factions eventually tend to form two antagonistic fronts, one of which is typically the governing side while another is the opposition, and often clash in a civil war, unless the groups cannot come to terms about power sharing. In the latter scenario, the involvement of external powers plays a critical role. When issues cannot be resolved by non-violent means various political, ethnic, and religious factions tend to mingle together forming two antagonistic fronts, thereby reflecting the duality of the identity and humankind.

Doyle maintains that,

> although there is no perfect solution to the problem of implementing human values on a global scale, the Kantian liberal peace lays claim to being the optimal combination, the one that gets us the most peace and global prosperity at the least cost in liberty, independence, and the least trampling on national identities.[21]

The Kantian notion of a liberal peace achieved on the global scale through the promotion of liberal democratic regimes is limited in so far as what one might view as non-democratic is, in fact, a democracy at its best, not the least bit different from any other. What one might call an "independent" democracy is viewed by another as autocracy. However, at the core of all political processes lies the struggle for power between two identity groups as demonstrated by a dyadic nature of both the political rivalries and military confrontations. In light of these tendencies, current understandings of western democratic rule and its separation from non-democratic politics is erroneous since all regimes that come to power do so through popular support, whether a popular vote or a revolution. As a result of the electoral process one group always ends up to preside over another through the presidential power. It is, therefore, appropriate to conclude that all political systems are democratic in so far as the groups that come to power do so through popular support which is expressed in different forms, whether a revolution or an electoral process. Democracies in their general shape and content tend to resemble in all kinds and settings. The difference is in that different identity groups have unique conceptions of democracy, corresponding to their intrinsic values and perceptions of human liberty and an ideal social organization. A liberal identity group espouses values that may be vastly different from those worshipped by a conservative group. Western democracies have an established record of supporting movements representing people of non-traditional sexual orientations. In particular, the majority of populations in the West support such movements prompting governments to promote policies which nurture the growth of political and socio-cultural diversity, whereas countries of the so called conservative camp have consistently rejected such values with outright criticism. In addition, western liberal democracies hardly ever have recognized the legitimacy of the leadership in Russia and the Soviet Union, which likewise comes to power through popular support and is not the least bit less democratic than that of any western polity. A liberal and a conservative concept of democracy conflict in so far as the two identity groups have vastly different understandings of human liberty and an ideal social order.

Persons of all creeds have only several fundamental lifetime needs, namely, freedom, security, and opportunity for personal growth, whose achievement depends on whether a person is rightly positioned in geo-spatial terms, which explains the occurrence of human mobility throughout millennia. It is thus erroneous to view liberty as an absolute category. Rather, liberty is a highly relativistic notion which means that various identity groups have vastly different interpretations of it and, correspondingly, divergent policies with respect to constructing democracy which explains the antagonisms among the distinctive communities defined by ethnicity, nationality, religion, and other identity markers.

Even modern liberal democratic polities suffer from the internal power struggle between various political groups that in the end tend to form two confrontational fronts, whether during the presidential elections or prior to war. During the final stages of the presidential elections, only two leading candidates always appear to be leading the race for power in any given polity, reflecting the fact that the two major competing groups strive to achieve a dominant position within and beyond a state system. The ultimate reason why identity groups struggle for power is that by securing a dominant position they can achieve a higher chance of winning the space over which the identity groups struggled for millennia. Despite the fact that the contenders may come to terms with respect to how to facilitate power-sharing, the win-win scenario is impossible in the context of a struggle for space between the identity groups since one party always ends up to preside over another owing to a "monocratic" nature of political power - that is, there is always one ruler, i.e., a country president or a king, depending on how much power and potential each identity group is able to exert at any given point in time vis-à-vis the adversary group. That power is most clearly expressed in population preponderance, power potential and foreign support received from the overlapping identity group.

In the United Stated, there exist a myriad of political parties and movements, yet only two political parties always turn out to lead the race for power, namely, a Democratic and a Republican Party. Both parties reflect the constituency of the American people. Once a new regime comes to power representing either of the two identity groups, it usually sets out to promote policies that are geared to accommodate the interests and needs of predominantly their respective constituency, not that of an opponent party notwithstanding the *de jure* prevalence of constitutionalism and citizenship rights. The Republican Party tends to advance the interests of the wealthy classes and spearhead stringent foreign policies, while the Democratic government is usually prone to support the middle class and to promote rather flexible foreign policies.

Different identity groups that come to power in modern nation states through the electoral process tend to facilitate different policies with respect to relations with other countries and create domestic policies that address the needs of specific social classes representing an overlapping identity group. For example, Iran had at once good relations with the US during the reign of the Shah but after the outbreak of the Islamic Revolution the bilateral relations have deteriorated extensively. A similar pattern has followed the US-Cuba relations since the Cuban Revolution. US-Russian relations had experienced a short period of warming, also known as the "Reset", during the presidency of Dmitri Medvedev but have worsened extensively after Putin took up his third term as Russian president. The George W. Bush administration promoted policies that were vastly different from the policies facilitated during the presidency of his predecessor, Bill Clinton. That is to say, the former facilitated more belligerent foreign policy while the latter exhibited more flexibility and ability to compromise in domestic and foreign affairs. Both presidents represented distinct political parties and thus various social and identity groups since as a general rule the majority of constituency rarely shifts sides. Most people tend to be consistent in terms of their political views and backing of political parties throughout the span of their lifetime.

Even democratically-elected regimes can and often do value bi-partisanship second to unilateralism domestically, since their main concern is related to self-interest, which is in turn related to prosperity and well-being of their constituency and the corresponding identity group, not that of an opponent identity. That interest is related to self-survival of the identity group which can only be achieved through the territorial dominance. Thus, even liberal democratic regimes are beset by factionalism, special-interest lobbying, contestation for space and political power struggle between two antagonistic groups. Constitutionalism is imperative since it provides a rational-legal framework for the struggle thereby transforming it into a form of a constructive competition between the antagonistic identity groups and individuals representing distinct identities. One cannot guarantee, or, better to say, no one can guarantee a perpetual peace when the identities advance self-interest at the expense of another group's wellbeing. Thus, the role of constitutionalism is significantly eroded by the existence of various regionalisms produced by the identity alignment as individuals often cannot take advantage of their natural rights in the absence of the alignment with a dominant identity group which impels them to migrate to other locales in an effort to constitute a majority. According to English philosopher John Locke, those rights include "life, liberty, and estate".[22] Individuals whose identity does not resemble a dominant group in any given socio-political community are generally placed at a disadvantage when it comes to the realization of their natural, or inherent, rights such as these as they are naturally subjected to practices aimed at their exclusion or even elimination which explains multiple cases of mass deportation and mass murder perpetrated by certain identity groups against adversaries. That means that they are essentially deprived of their inherent rights.

According to the US Declaration of Independence, "We hold these truths to be self-evident, that all men are created equal, that they are endowed by their Creator with certain unalienable Rights..."[23] However, why can't an individual take advantage of his natural rights in any and all locales, but is constantly compelled to pursue those rights only in "suitable" communities, namely, those whose aligning identity group constitutes a majority?

In addition to that, the existence and significance of the transnational identity bonds overrides such classical concepts as the social contract theory proposed by such philosophers as Thomas Hobbes, Jean Jacques Rousseau, John Locke and Immanuel Kant whereby individuals, whether explicitly or tacitly, convey their personal liberty, at least part of it, to an overarching authority, a sovereign (i.e., the rule of law), which can guarantee them collective security in the framework of the nation state. According to French political philosopher Jean Jacques Rousseau,

> As soon as this multitude is united in one body, you cannot offend one of its members without attacking the body; much less can you offend the body without incurring the resentment of all the members.[24]

Individuals make rational and political choices in accordance with their views with respect to individual and common interests which derive from their belonging to a certain identity group since their welfare is intimately connected to the welfare of persons closely connected to them in terms of their group affiliation. But the bonds between individuals cannot be forged spontaneously since social groups tend to form not randomly, or subject to presence of common interest. Rather, the presence or absence of common interest is related to peoples' innate shared links of allegiance defined in terms of the identity.

Constitutionalism, which sets up a framework for social order and a respect of individual liberty and dignity, can likewise be seen as a relativistic notion along the lines of different interpretations of liberty among the distinctive identity groups. Despite the relative similarity of constitutionalisms in various geo-political settings, identity groups always tend to create new forms of constitutionalism or adapt old ones in order to suit to their particularistic needs, strategies of winning the space and promotion of dominance over the opponent identity group. That trend is exemplified by a general practice among the newly-formed governments to advance new policies related to defense, economy, social welfare, political transparency, and foreign affairs through the adoption of new legislative initiatives and procedures.

> In fact, each individual may, as a man, have a private will, dissimilar or contrary to the general will which he has as a citizen. His own private interest may dictate to him very differently from the common interest; his absolute and naturally independent existence may make him regard what he owes to the common cause as a gratuitious contribution, the omission of which would be less injurious to others than the payment would be burdensome to himself; and considering the moral person which constitutes the State as a creature of the imagination, because it is not a man, he may wish to enjoy the rights of a citizen without being disposed to fulfill the duties of a subject. Such an injustice would in its progress cause the ruin of the body politic. [25]

Since persons can only be affiliated with and promote the interests of their respective overlapping identity group not that of the opponent party, groups in power always represent a certain identity group, not a populace in its entirety. Constitutionalism sets up a framework for order and a respect of human dignity in societies, but it must be seen as a relativistic concept in a situation when human identities by their nature always seek to advance their particularistic interests even in constitutional democracies whose goal is to provide a foundation for peaceful coexistence, equality, and cooperation among the contending identity groups.

> a social contract theory is one that maintains that governments come into existence through the contract or agreement of certain parties. Usually the contract is understood to be between a sovereign and his subjects. [26]
> The sovereign controls all the political power there is in the government, and he has authority to control every aspect of life. This entails that a sove-

reign cannot act unjustly towards a subject, because everything the sovereign
does is authorized by the subject; "and consequently he that complaineth of
injury from his sovereign complaineth of that whereof he himself is author;
and therefore [he] ought not to accuse any man but himself." [27]

As representative governments can only be elected by the majority of the
population, which is far from being absolute in a vast majority of cases, it can
hardly be possible in electoral democracies that anyone can only accuse
oneself for the misdemeanor of a sovereign, since that sovereign can only be
placed in power by two votes in favor and one vote against it. Democratically
elected regimes always represent a majority, but by far not the entire population of a nation state but so do the governments that rise to power through
revolutions. Thus, revolutions are as democratic as free elections are. Inter-
estingly enough, revolutions are still considered illegitimate.

Given a dyadic nature of political competition and a "monocratic" nature
of civil governments and high public office, it is a fact that there always
exists a bold separation line between those that rule and those being ruled.
Those in power tend to promote the interests of their respective constituency
and the identity group, not that of the opponent group. For instance, why
different governments tend to promote various and often contradictory policies on same issues such as the economy, defense, business, foreign trade,
international relations, taxes, political lobbying and campaigning? Some political leaders may prioritize the welfare of the middle class, servicemen,
senior citizens, while others can nurture the corporatist interests and those of
the wealthy citizens.

Locke describes legitimate government as an impartial judge or umpire.
Government, properly structured, can be disinterested, dispassionate, non-par-
tisan. It is the impartiality of such a government that allows Locke to characterize it both as rational and free government. [28]

Given a dyadic nature of societies and a continued importance of nation-
states in the global system, process of contestation for political power between two political fronts representing two human identities allows only one
group at a time to occupy high public office. Liberal and conservative propo-
sitions for extensive power sharing agreements are thus oftentimes rendered
inadequate since no power sharing agreement can accommodate both groups
in high public office, such as a country president. That is to say, only one
person can hold a position of a country president at a time. A power sharing
agreement at best can only provide a second-level position to another con-
testant and the identity group behind it, i.e., that of a prime minister. Modern
understanding of power exerted on an international scale is limited in so far
as it does not account for the overwhelming role of transnational identity
bonds among the identity groups which take advantage of the national and

international mechanisms of social regulation to advance their innate interest related to propagation. The power of transnational identity bonds is a principal factor influencing the outcome of political contestation within and beyond the national polities. Those identity linkages transcend the boundaries of political and legal entities set to contain them.

Process of migration exemplifies the process of a power struggle within countries whereby overlapping identities are constantly being expanded through incoming migration flows while adversary groups are being subjected to the expulsion policies of those set to dominate in polities. It is these policies that lead to out-migration of the identity groups into other localities where they seek to coalesce with the overlapping identity in order to constitute a majority. Thus, migration processes are an integral part of a power struggle between the antagonistic identity groups which occurs in polities for millennia. It is the support and resources of overlapping identity groups that determine the outcome of a power struggle in favor of a stronger party in any given polity during the electoral process.

Classical realism stresses the human nature to dominate as a cause of war subject to ego and emotion of world leaders. In particular, Morgenthau argues that "politics is governed by objective laws that have their roots in human nature"[29] However, such categories as "good states" and "bad states", i.e., "good state behavior" and "bad state behavior" are quite ambiguous in light of the fact that various identity groups that hold power in nation states tend to advance divergent moral concepts and thereby interpretations of good behavior *vis-à-vis* other states since in international relations much emphasis is made on whether or not an aligning identity group holds power in another state. In that case, overlapping identity groups interpret their conduct as good relative to that of an adversary group and vice versa. States tend to shift their alliances depending on whether or not groups in power have the support of overlapping identity groups in other countries. Process of identity alignment has a great effect on state behavior and state interactions. Cooperation in economic, political and military affairs often depends not so much on perceptions of absolute gain, or a pursuit of best deals, as on the presence or absence of the identity bonds among the regimes in countries which can guarantee both the former and the latter.

NOTES

1. According to Samuel Huntington, the author of the clash of civilizations hypothesis, the main conflict in the world will occur between different civilizations. In particular, he argues that the fundamental source of conflict will not be economic or ideological, but a cultural one. The main conflict will occur between nations and groups of different civilizations. Huntington differentiated between the Western civilization, the Orthodox world of the former Soviet Union, the Latin American world, the Eastern civilization, the Muslim world, and the Civilization of sub-Saharan Africa.

2. Kant, Immanuel. *Perpetual Peace: A Philosophical sketch*, 1795, pp. 13-16.

3. Ibid.

4. Ibid.

5. Danilovic, Vesna and Clare, Joe. "The Kantian Liberal Peace (Revisited)," *American Journal of Political Science*, Vol. 51, No. 2, 2007, pp. 397-414.

6. See, for instance, Aristotle. *Politics: A Treatise on Government.*

7. Eisenberg, Myron G., Cynthia Griggins, and Richard J. Duval. Disabled People as Second-Class Citizens, Vol. 2, (New York: Springer), 1982.

8. See, for instance, studies on the role of Diasporas in shaping domestic political processes.

9. Article Two of the United States Constitution.

10. Locke, John. *Second Treatise of Government*, Edited by Macpherson, C.B., (Hackett Publishing), 1980, pp. 52-53.

11. Ibid.

12. Ibid.

13. Krasner, Stephen and Pascual, Carlos. "Addressing State Failure," *Foreign Affairs*, 156, 2005.

14. Elliot, Larry. "Russia's entry to WTO ends 19 years of negotiations," 2012, Source: http://www.theguardian.com/business/economics-blog/2012/aug/22/russia-entry-world-trade-organisation.

15. Garthoff, Raymond. "Détente and Confrontation: American-Soviet Relations from Nixon to Regan," Final report to the National Council for Soviet and East-European Research, (The Brookings Institution), 1982.

16. Osman, Tarek. *Egypt on the Brink: From Nasser to Mubarak*, (Yale University Press), 2011, p. 67.

17. Burgess, John. "Orthodox Resurgence", *The Christian Century*, 2009, pp. 25-28. http://search.proquest.libraryproxy.griffith.edu.au/docview/217269564?accountid=14543.

18. Ibid.

19. Doyle, Michael. *Liberal Peace: Selected Essays*, 1nd Edition, (Routledge), 2011, p. 167.

20. Ibid., p. 167.

21. Ibid., p. 167.

22. Locke, John. *Two Treaties of Government*, 1689.

23. Declaration of Independence of the United States of America. Source: http://www.archives.gov/exhibits/charters/declaration_transcript.html.

24. Rousseau, Jean. *The Social Contract*, 1762, p. 17.

25. Ibid., p. 18.

26. Martinich, A. *Hobbes*, 1st Edition, (Routledge), 2005, p. 54.

27. Ibid., p. 129.

28. Grant, Ruth. *John Locke's Liberalism Reconsidered*, (University of Chicago Press), 1987, p. 180.

29. Morgenthau, H. J. *Politics Among Nations: The Struggles for Power and Peace* (Brief Edition), McGraw-Hill Higher Education: Boston, 1992, p. 4.

Chapter One

Human Liberty in the Context of Identity Alignment

Only when individuals are properly positioned geographically and in terms of their respective identity groups can they freely pursue opportunities for personal and social realization. Process of identity alignment determines one's access to opportunities for personal and social achievement, namely, education, employment and social integration. Thus, human mobility is a direct result of an individual's pursuit of the identity alignment whereby people situated in locales where a divergent identity group dominates are compelled to pursue such opportunities in different settings through the process of migration. It is these inherent policies of the identity groups aimed at the homogenization of space that drive the migration processes. Conversely, communities are in a constant pursuit of an internal cohesion through the process of homogenization and absorption of overlapping groups migrating from other places. In a similar vein, human liberty and the prospect of realization of one's citizenship and inherent rights depend on whether a person is rightly positioned in terms of the alignment with the overlapping identity group whose purpose is to secure and maximize control over space through the identity homogeneity and territorial dominance. Thus, individuals in a position of a minority are often denied opportunities to realize their most basic rights such the ability to freely cast votes, or to acquire the basic instruments of social influence such as employment and education, thereby subjected to social forces aimed at exclusion and expulsion. Having employment guarantees the individual the rights and privileges to which a person is entitled by the constitution which, in turn, depends on a suitability of a person in any particular locale. If not, individuals are *de facto* being deprived of those natural rights, such as a right to employment, education, and residence, and, as such, the right to life, by the majority identity group which

29

seeks to dominate across space by means of the homogenization and exclusion of an alien identity group.

It is thus appropriate to assert that it is only with the achievement of alignment that individuals can have the potential to bring to fruition their lifetime goals and realize their inherent virtues, for a person positioned in a community where a distinctive identity group plays a dominant role is naturally placed at a disadvantage relative to members of a prevailing group. Consequently, the role of overarching human rights is significantly eroded by the existence of informal practices underlying the identity bonds. This is exemplified by high levels of intolerance toward individuals who espouse divergent political and socio-cultural views when they are positioned in a certain community. That is to say, a conservative migrant has slim chances of migrating to the West, whereas a liberal one is not only is able to do so but is also equipped with virtues to achieve a high level professional realization owing to a convergence of the identity linkages with the dominant identity group. A person of non-traditional sexual orientation is likely to be subjected to various forms of discriminatory treatment and stigmatization if he or she is positioned in a certain community characterized by traditional and conservative worldviews. Yet, persons of a non-traditional sexual orientation portray the highest level of expression of the identity affiliation. People with lower levels of expression can similarly be subjected to discrimination and stigmatization, if they are positioned in a distinctive identity group.

Chapter Two

From Individual to Social Regionalism

Conflict within Societies and Provoked Mobility

CAUSES OF MIGRATION

I argue that migration processes are driven by such factors as provoked mobility, which occurs when certain groups are subjected to practices of discrimination aimed at expulsion or subjugation by the majority identity group. Process of provoked mobility derives from the majority identity's strategy of maximizing a territorial dominance through the expulsion of an alien identity group. I addition, I stress the role of the identity bonds which sustain migration flows. Migrants from certain nations tend to travel only to countries where similar identities hold the greatest amount of leverage in political, economic, administrative, and cultural terms.

That is to say, I argue that countries that are ruled by a conservative identity tend to send migrants to countries where a similar identity holds power. For instance, Chinese migrants are prone to work in countries like Malaysia or Singapore, the US and Australia where the Chinese diasporas constitute a significant share of the population. Likewise, migrants from India, Pakistan and Bangladesh tend to work in the oil-rich nations of the Persian Gulf whose indigenous population is aligned with them in terms of the identity. Countries where a liberal identity constitutes a majority and thus holds a significant degree of power only accept migrants that are linked to them in terms of the identity. While provoked mobility plays a central role in providing the push force for the migration, the need to bolster the territorial dominance of the identities in the receiving countries plays a key role in the migration pull force.

31

Regionalisms are sustained through inter-generational continuity and the policies of the identity groups aimed at the homogenization. Regional identities create nationalist frameworks for adjusting a collective mindset, behavior, create a new ideology in order to seclude it from the contending identities, such as when setting behavioral and fashion standards within different institutions and locales in efforts to conform them to a collective perception of an ideal community order and the nationalist agenda. This inevitably produces internal conflict owing to the fact that societies have a dyadic nature. Behavioral homogenization involves the imposition of informal and formal social and legal norms by the dominant identity to standardize collective behavior and to conform to its nationalist agenda. Often, coercion and lack of gradualism in social transformation lead to outbreak of conflicts, which is generally the case after a coup and possible repressions by one identity in order to contain the dissent of another group.

I argue that both in- and out-migration is a product of the homogenization processes in societies, rather than simply economic, political, and other motivations considered in many studies on migration.[1] Most modern studies focus on migration in the context of the receiving countries of the developed "North" and generally developing polities of the global "South" and the nexus between development and migration. The alternating order of the combination "North-South" reflects the diversity of migratory flows worldwide, according to that stance.[2]

My hypothesis stresses the roles of the identity bonds among various states and regions, rather than various economic areas of the world. What is more important in that context is why Indian migrants tend to search for better life and work venues in some countries and not in others, while Chinese migrants look for employment only in nations that are linked to them in terms of the identity and culture, for instance, Singapore, Russia, and Malaysia? Identity bonds have a great effect on migration patterns, which sustain world regionalisms. Migrants from certain nations tend to travel only to countries where similar identities hold the greatest amount of leverage in political, economic, administrative and cultural terms.

TERRITORIAL DOMINANCE

The policies of the identity groups aimed at reinforcing the homogeneity create situations of instability and tension within societies, especially when there are limited ways to escape the social or political pressures for the minority groups, through out-migration or political bargaining. There is a perennial struggle between a conservative and a liberal identity within societies. In this book, the object of their struggle is termed a *territorial dominance*. Groups that seek power do so in order to maximize their control over land and resources, increase their dominance within a society and across space. They seek to coalesce with overlapping identities in an effort to expand territorially, by excluding an alien identity from within the territorial domain over which they seek to establish or maximize control.

They seek to increase their influence both qualitatively and quantitatively, that is, through the predominance and competition. Since the concept of democracy provides a legal-rational legitimatization for the rule of the majority, it becomes all the more important in a contestation for space, which is a struggle for supremacy by all means. Democracy simply becomes a justification for the dominance of the majority identity group. All in all, the ultimate goal for the identity is to maximize its influence and presence across space. As an individual human being possesses an inherent need for space, so it is the very purpose of the identities to occupy space and to extend their influence across territories, which explains the persistence of the regionalisms, conflicts between individuals within societies and between the identities on a wider scale.

The conflict between identities within societies usually has a concealed form - that is, before it either breaks out into an outright civil war or the contenders come to understand the importance of sharing power. Conflict is concealed in so far as the groups in power seek to retain their legitimacy at an international level and as part of the global economic system. However, the ramifications of the conflict can be easily identified in the migration patterns that are taking place, whereby some groups with defined shared characteristics such as a regional association, religion, or ethnicity, are compelled to migrate abroad in search of better work and life options. Meanwhile, other groups of populace sharing appropriate traits not migrating to the extent as the former do. In this book, this process is referred to as *provoked mobility*, which occurs as a result of the subjection to concealed discrimination by the majority identity groups which possess a significant access to political power, financial institutions and instruments of coercion. Among people who espouse liberal worldviews are those of a non-traditional sexual orientation who are routinely subjected to structural discrimination by the majority identities which espouse more traditional, conservative worldviews, specifically, with respect to issues of sexuality and various forms of personal expression.

Thus, even countries built on conventional notions of liberal democratic rule and social equality promote policies that are principally favorable to the majority identity, whereby minorities often become victims of mainstream political thinking and decision-making process. For example, Doyle and Molix note that "attitudes towards sexual minorities in the United States tend to be unfavorable. This negativity towards sexual minorities is perpetuated at a structural level. A number of different public policies in the United States actively discriminate against sexual minorities (e.g. the Defense of Marriage Act) and can result in increased perceptions of stigma and impaired health and well-being among gay men and lesbian women."[3] It is important to note that among people of so-called non-traditional sexual orientations or unconventional ways of thinking are those excluded from socialization processes engendered by the majorities through stigmatization and the creation of social-cultural barriers to self-realization.

Regionally-defined identity groups seek to achieve a complete dominance over space via the expulsion or subjugation of an alien identity group. Informal practices and control over institutions of power constitute the core of the exclusion and subjugation strategies. The main strategy underlying the identity groups' propagation policy is to occupy key leadership and executive positions in the state system and gradually transform it into an instrument of dominance and homogenization of space. While alien identity is not expelled outright, it becomes a part of the repression system which is aimed at it. Identities that are not aligned with a dominating group are subjected to various forms of discrimination, such as rejection of job candidates, depriving the right to residence, providing low quality services and consumer products, creation of multiple social barriers and stigmatization on the basis of identity features such as race or ethnicity. Practices of social exclusion so common in such cases lead to the provoked mobility phenomenon.

To achieve a territorial dominance, identities set out to strengthen their position by restricting employment and social opportunities to a distinct identity group, thereby creating fertile ground to a provoked mobility. Contrary to economic motives, which, according to many studies lead to out-migration, practices of structural discrimination and social exclusion have a direct impact on a process of provoked mobility. The circumstances which compel people to seek better jobs and life opportunities abroad are a product of informal policies and concealed discrimination aimed at the expulsion of an alien identity. This includes restricting employment and social inclusion to members of an alien identity group so as to minimize its propagation of power and presence across space. It is a crucial aspect of the identities' homogenization strategies. Identities occupy space and their prime goal is to inhibit the propagation of an alien identity group, thereby securing the control over land and resources.

An important aspect of homogenization policies of identities derives from a perception of whether an individual fits into the wider political-societal milieu. Alien identity is subjected to various forms of societal rejection. Members of distinct identities often cannot take full advantage of their citizenship rights and freedoms; acquire adequate expertise and education for realization of their personal and career objectives. Others who are employed are often denied career promotion on the grounds of not being fit in a specific locale and institution. It is important to note that modern forms of discriminatory treatment are generally concealed in so far as the dominant identity group seeks to retain the legitimacy and recognition by groups situated in other locales, yet the pattern of exclusion of an alien identity group is consistent with widespread discriminatory practices.

Schulze examines the expulsion of the German populations from their traditional homelands in central, eastern, and south-eastern Europe after the end of the Second World War. He notes that from 12 to 14 million Germans were affected by the compulsory relocation policies as part of the efforts to construct a new German polity, the West and East Germany that was by then exposed to the influence of the two global powers representing a conservative and a liberal identity.[4] There are other notable examples of enforced relocation of certain ethnic, religious, or national groups resulting from non-alignment matters. For instance, in a process of constructing a Soviet polity, the new ruling elites resorted to a similar strategy of relocating certain groups defined by race, ethnicity, religion, or regional affiliation to other locales. One example is mass deportation of over 500,000 Chechen, Ingush, Balkar, Karachays, Circassians, Meskhetian Turks, Crimean Tatars and other groups to Central Asia during the Second World War by the Soviet leadership on alleged cooperation with the Nazi Germany. Tragic events of such kind often associated with mass deaths and deportation inevitably become instilled in the ethos of countries that juxtapose them with competing identities and further prolong the hostility for decades, if not centuries. They also become a focal point of history discourses that are used to ignite and augment the ideological confrontation between contentious nation-states and ethnic groups.

Another notable case is the deportation of the Armenians, Assyrians and Greeks in the Ottoman Empire during the reign of Sultan Abdul Hamid II and especially during the rule of the Young Turk's regime at the dawn of the 20th century. The ultimate goal of mass deportation of populations is to rid a new polity of the "unfit" groups which is usually followed or accompanied by mass killing. The genocide of the Armenians perpetrated by the Young Turks regime is one of the most notable examples as is the industrialized campaign of exterminating the "unfit" ethnic and racial groups by the Nazi regime in Germany. Estimations of the number of people killed in the Ottoman Empire during the so called death marches and other acts of mass killing vary from 1 million to 1.5 million. Those targeted were the Christian populations of the Ottoman Empire: the Armenians, the Assyrians, and the Greeks.

It is through the deportation of an alien group that identities promote a policy of territorial dominance. Cases of structural discrimination and mass murder of population groups defined by race, ethnicity, nationality, or religious affiliation exemplify the last stages of a strategy of the identity groups aimed at maximizing their territorial dominance. The earlier stages include application of structural discrimination that were particularly widespread during the period of the colonialism, prior to the advent of globalism and the rise of international human rights institutions and conventions to which the vast majority of states are now signatories.

When identities promote a policy of segregation and seclusion, they inevitably produce a class of social outcasts that have no ways to remedy the situation whatsoever and are doomed to the desperate existence. Denied access to proper education and employment opportunities, people often rely on social welfare payments and donations for survival, with members of the ruling identity group occupying the vast majority of the administrative and leadership positions in the socio-economic system. For instance, the developed countries of the west have generally been dubbed welfare states, countries, where social dissent is constantly satiated by the myriads of welfare programs for the underprivileged societal strata. It is a product of the identity's homogenization strategy aimed at the propagation of dominance across space and is the essence of concealed discrimination.

The modern welfare state is based on the identities' in power policy of appeasement whereby they can quench the dissent of the opposing identity group through budgetary allocations in order to sustain a territorial dominance and avoid civil strife, since those underprivileged are generally subjected to the wider societal rejection through social alienation and deprivation of opportunities for personal realization and social integration. In addition, member nations of the Organization for Economic Cooperation and Development (OECD) have high levels of political freedom and transparency which are essential for enabling those in vulnerable or underprivileged positions to seek redress via most accessible free public services and institutions; whereas, in countries with low levels of transparency and absence of impartial constitutionalism, only the most vulnerable social strata mainly representing a minority identity group are deprived of access to fundamental public institutions and services and are thus denied the realization of their inherent rights.

Different identity groups in power tend to promote different social welfare policies. Currently, there are different types of welfare states according to the nature of their policies on the distribution of benefits among the population. Some welfare states may be liberal in nature, dominated by the logic of the market; others may be conservative/corporatism welfare states where benefits tend to be stratified.[5] The third welfare state type is the social democratic. This type is based on universalism and the "usurpation" of the market. It is based on the idea of public responsibility for individual welfare and universal access to social services and supports.[6] One's approach to social welfare programs can be driven by such factors as particularistic judgments concerning the distribution of assets among different societal strata occupied by various identity groups. Some groups defined by the identity may hold the leadership positions in any given country and occupy the highest social strata, while others may occupy midlevel sectors and fulfill secondary responsibilities in the state hierarchy. This explains the existence of differential approaches by actors to state policies such as social welfare, a prioritization of certain state policies and target groups over others.

Civil wars erupt when opportunities to escape various forms of concealed structural discrimination and coercive dominance imposed by the identities in power are very limited or absent. They include out-migration, political consensus, power-sharing agreements, and concessions by the dominant identity to provide better opportunities for personal realization and social integration to members of a distinctive identity group. Civil wars break out between a state party, which generally represents a majority in the population and a minority group fighting as the opposing party. The main motive behind rebel fighting is to undermine the system of dominance of the majority identity group and to transform it either into its own dominance instrument or to reach a consensus about a power-sharing based on a principle of equitable distribution of power. Both civil and world wars occur when a confrontation between a conservative and a liberal identity reaches an apex point. In other words, conflicts between the identity groups erupt when circumstances surrounding the struggle do not accommodate a peaceful resolution, while only a violent confrontation is seen by both parties as the optimal form of solution.

NOTES

1. According to modern studies, economic opportunities, economic degradation, violence, political and religious oppression, and economic development are the main factors driving migration. See, for instance, Stutz, Christa. "Migration." In *Encyclopedia of Human Geography*, edited by Warf, Barney. 302-4. (Thousand Oaks, CA: SAGE Publications, Inc.), 2006. (http://dx.doi.org.libraryproxy.griffith.edu.au/10.4135/9781412952422.n184)

2. According to data provided by the UN DESA, in 2010, the South-North migration flows constituted the majority (45%) of total world migration, followed by South-South (35%), North-North (17%), North-South (3%).The scale of North-South migration varies according to various sources from 13 million by the United Nations Department of Economic and Social Affairs (UN DESA) measures to 7 million according to the World Bank and the UNDP calculations. The numbers for South-South also vary from 87 million according to the UNDP calculations to 75-73 according to the UN DESA and the World Bank. The South-North accounts for 95 million migrants according to the World Bank, and 87 and 74 million according to the UNDP and UN DESA estimations, respectively. Another interesting observation is contained in the Gallup report which suggests that North-North migrants tend to be more affluent financially than migrants travelling from South to North, North to South, or South to South.

3. Doyle, David and Molix, Lisa. "Perceived Discrimination and Well-Being in Gay Men: The Protective Role of Behavioral Identification," *Psychology & Sexuality*, Vol. 5, Iss. 2, 2014, p. 117.

4. Schulze, Rainer. The Politics of Memory: Flight and Expulsion of German Populations after the Second World War and German Collective Memory, *National Identities*, Vol. 8, Iss. 4, 2006, p. 367.

5. Pankratz, Curt. "Welfare State Regimes and the Evolution of Liberalism," *Journal of International and Comparative Social Policy*, 2014, p. 3.

6. Ibid.

Chapter Three

Fragmented Families

All nations and regions of the world are divided along the lines of the identity duality notwithstanding the stringency of the homogenization policies of the identity groups in power due to a critical aspect termed *the fragmentation of families*. It occurs along the lines of the identity duality and results in a regionalism, provoked mobility, and conflicts, from a family level and further to state and region. As a general rule, the fragmentation occurs between parents and children. If a fragmentation of families takes place, it entails a process of separation, divorce and further to regionalisms since those family members that eventually separate tend to move further away from their relatives in order to coalesce with overlapping identity groups and to extend their presence to other areas. In case when family members separate from their indigenous locales and coalesce with overlapping identity groups, they can achieve a higher chance of a personal realization and social integration since they are more likely to be recognized by the overlapping identity group. In the course of history, this has proven to be relevant in light of the colonization of either uninhabited areas or those inhabited by both overlapping indigenous identity groups and not that were technologically weaker than the invading ones. People were driven out of their indigenous localities by the invading identity groups and their armies, a process that bears a striking resemblance to modern day migration and a process of provoked mobility except that it has acquired a more civilized pattern. Overall, this process follows a cyclic pattern as identity groups tend to shift their positions of being a majority in any given locale and polity. Absence or lack of opportunities for one's social integration or achievement of economic sufficiency in the indigenous locale plays a key role in the migration push force. Simultaneously, the need to expand the dominance of the identity group compels it to attract overlapping groups from other locales.

Family members whose identities overlap tend to live in close proximity to each other. The process of fragmentation of families constitutes the foundation of world regionalisms, which are, in turn, a source of all conflicts. As the confrontation of identities, the fragmentation of families is a crucial aspect of human nature whose main effect is the propagation and conflict of identities for space. The fragmentation of families results from both marriages between the divergent identities and homogenous unions, that is, where the identities of spouses are properly aligned. Families in such scenarios tend to be fragmented between spouses and children, as well as among siblings. This partly demonstrates a causal link between divorce and absence of the identity alignment. The process of divorce inevitably involves matters related to the division of property and illustrates conflicts of personal regionalisms since properties are an integral part of one's acquired personal domain and locale. The fact that females can make claims on the males' properties as a result of a divorce is an indication of a female's significance in providing attachment to space for males, which likewise underpins the policy of granting citizenship to newborns in all countries of the world. Finzi-Dottan and Cohen conducted a study of predictors of sibling's relations among 202 young adults. They conclude that:

> one of the roots of warmth and conflict in adult sibling relations can be traced to the developmental effects of the perception of having been treated differently by the parents in comparison with a sibling. Such perceptions affect one's evaluation of oneself as worthy or unworthy of parental attention and may also affect one's level of narcissism.[1]

It is important to highlight that there is a tendency for families to fragment among parents and siblings which raises questions about the causal factors as well as the outcomes of the fragmented families. Yet, the real reason why families fragment has to be sought in a personal and family regionalism phenomenon and aligning identity groups within families, which produce expulsions of alien ones. Since it is difficult to account for the consistency in a pattern of youngest siblings being favored by parents, other factors must be considered as well. Identity alignments can provide some explanation as to why families fracture.

World regionalisms are a product of provoked mobility, coercive dominance of the identities, various forms of structural discrimination, and the fragmentation of families. The dominant identity's concealed policy of structural discrimination is prevalent in all societies across the world, no matter whether the country is developed economically or is undergoing a transition period as those aspects of social fragmentation, namely, the identity dichotomy and the fragmentation of families constitute the core of human nature.

Migration patterns across the planet tend to resemble despite the relative differences in the political systems among sending and receiving countries. Whereas only when countries are politically allied do they tend to cooperate on migration matters, migration patterns remain significantly identical in all corners of the world. According to the accepted argument migration takes place when there is a demand for labor force in the receiving countries and a supply of force in the sending countries.[2] My argument stresses the role of the identity bonds that sustain migration flows from one country to another across the world. In particular, I argue that countries that are ruled by a conservative identity tend to send migrants to countries where a similar identity holds power. For instance, Chinese migrants are prone to work in countries like Malaysia or Singapore, the US and Australia where the Chinese diasporas and aligning groups constitute a significant share of the population. Likewise, migrants from India, Pakistan and Bangladesh tend to work in the oil-rich nations of the Persian Gulf whose indigenous population is aligned with them in terms of the identity. Countries where a liberal identity constitutes a majority and thus holds a significant degree of power tend to send migrants to countries that are linked to them in terms of the identity. Provoked mobility plays a central role in providing the push force for migration while the need to increase the territorial dominance of identities in the receiving countries plays a key role in the migration pull force.

GENDER ROLES IN THE PROCESS OF REGIONALISM

Since females generally are much more closely tied to land than males, they are considered to be the "keepers" of territories and the identities since it has generally been the rule that females rarely migrate as opposed to males.[3] While it is important to account for the difference in the responsibilities among family members, the primary role of females is to maintain the identities and the territories occupied by them through socialization processes which they tend to control. While families are the building blocks of societies, females play a crucial role in the processes of family formation. Females create and sustain identity continuities through the selection of males that must fit into a certain social and political milieu. The role of males is largely related to safeguarding the identities and to the maintenance and expansion of the identities across space, which explains why predominantly males are engaged in combats. While males are the active participants of warfare, females are predominantly the passive ones.

It is demonstrative that females more often than not tend to live closer to their immediate families than males. Males are more prone to separation from families and to attachment to new places in line with their identity, which is why divorces are so common today among migrants who are prone to finding better attachment in places they migrate to. Gigy and Kelly found that the reasons for divorces are related to the "loss of closeness, and feelings of emotional bareness, boredom with the marriage, and serious differences in lifestyle and values."[4]

> Whereas women divorcing for reasons of a substance abusing spouse were more likely to distrust their spouses and report poor communication about their children, both men and women divorcing for reasons of unmet emotional needs/gradual growing apart.[5]

Clifford also finds a significant positive correlation between male migration and fertility processes in Tajikistan as females are rendered vulnerable to being subjected to various forms of stigmatization and cultural pressures resulting from such personal circumstances.[6] Furthermore, migrants' wives are highly prone to being subjected to discrimination by those in a more favorable position, which includes but is not limited to restricting access to proper job opportunities or working in adverse environmental conditions thereby leading to aggravating consequences for health, families, and societies. Children in migrant families quite often cannot attain sufficient levels of education and qualification so as to escape the cycle of poverty and are likewise destined to become migrants.

In harmonious marriages, that is, where spouses are properly aligned in terms of their identity group affiliation, cohabitation usually occurs without significant setbacks and disagreements throughout the span of marriage. It again underscores the significance placed on the identity alignment in a process of selection of partners. Quite often, problems related to substance abuse are a side-effect of non-alignment issues and their various manifestations such as a loss of interest and trust in a partner or recurring differences in life style. Cases of divorce always involve issues related to the distribution of property and specifically, real estate, which is a good case in point of the process of spousal regionalism. Drawing the invisible dividing lines by spouses in their living quarters is an early indication of unhealthy relationships, non-alignment and family regionalism.

While families are the building blocks of identities, it is the identities that construct societies and nations according to their perceptions of an ideal statehood and social organization. Once a new identity comes to power replacing another as a result of a violent take-over or otherwise supported by a foreign power, a whole new cycle of political and economic reforms usually comes to life which marks the commencement of a social restructuring process which often incurs violent measures against an alien identity group.

SOCIAL APPROVAL OF MARRIAGES

A salient aspect of marriage practices is what I termed *social approval of marriages*, a key element of the identities' strategy of territorial dominance and a pretext to a provoked mobility. Only those marriages are approved that are seen to expand any given identity group, while alien ones are disapproved through widespread stigmatization and imposition of social barriers. While the process of family formation is in itself an integral part of the identity's attempts at self-sustenance and propagation, understanding the process of social approval of marriages will enable us to understand the processes of community formation in which the identity bonds play a pivotal role.

Being prevalent in all societies of the world, the process of social approval of marriages is a key element of the processes which sustain and exacerbate world regionalisms. Space, or land, over which identities and individuals seek to maximize control and the mechanisms underlying the homogenization of identities, including the social approval of marriages is what drives human mobility. Those excluded from their indigenous locales tend to move to other places where they can coalesce with a prevalent identity group and thus achieve a higher degree of personal realization and social integration. Thus, an individual's chance of success is primarily dependent on the ability to find the right place, or, more precisely, the right commune, so as to avoid undermining the homogeneity of the indigenous identity and to contribute to the process of expansion of the overlapping one.

According to the 2010 World Bank data, a significant share of the population in such countries as Germany, Canada, the Russian Federation, the United States, Italy, Spain, and France constitute people who were born overseas. United States topped the list with more than 42 million immigrants, followed by Russia with nearly 12 million immigrants, Germany with 10 million, Spain with 6 million, Canada with 7 million, France with more than 6 million, India with more than 5 million, and Italy with more than 4 million immigrants.[7] Males are subjected to provoked mobility at much higher levels than females, because of the former's weaker connection to land than that of the latter. It is, therefore, appropriate to assume that females safeguard the identities, while males are primarily responsible for the expansion of identities across space.

While the separation of females from their immediate families is also commonplace, females play a critical role in the sustenance and proliferation of both a conservative and a liberal identity because of being in the right position to control the process of achieving a territorial dominance by the identity. For instance, in the majority of divorce cases, children stay with their mothers rather than fathers[8], while fathers separate, which, among other things, reflects the importance of a female's role in maintaining the continuity of identity groups and their strong attachment to land.

It has generally been the case that following the process of separation in families and the ensuing out-migration, families fragment further to the point when relations among members of the family deteriorate which exemplifies the prevalence of family fragmentation and its aggravating consequences. It serves as the basis of human mobility, human conflict and the expansion of human presence across space.

NOTES

1. Finzi-Dottan, Ricky and Cohen, Orna. "Young Adult Sibling Relations: The Effects of Perceived Parental Favoritism and Narcissism," *The Journal of Psychology*, Vol. 145, Iss.1, 2010, p. 15.

2. See, for instance, Bauer, T.K. and Zimmermann, K.F. *The Economics of Migration*, (Northampton, MA.), 2002.

3. According to the World Migration Report prepared by the International Organization for Migration in 2013, the majority of migrants worldwide are male. Female migrants constitute the majority of migrants only in the North-North direction of migratory flows, that is, only among the developed countries.

4. Gigy, Lynn and Kelly, Joan. "Reasons for Divorce: Perspectives of Divorcing Men and Women," *Journal of Divorce and Remarriage*, Vol. 18, Iss. 1-2, 1993.

5. Ibid., p. 185.

6. Clifford, David. "Spousal Separation, Selectivity and Contextual Effects: Exploring the Relationship Between International Labor Migration and Fertility in Post-Soviet Tajikistan," *Demographic Research*, Max Planck Institute for Demographic Research, Rostock, Germany, Vol. 21(32), 2009, pages 945-975.

7. United Nations Population Division, Trends in Total Migrant Stock: 2008 Revision, Source: http://data.worldbank.org/indicator/SM.POP.TOTL.

8. Galarneau, D. and Sturrock, J. Family Income after Separation. *Perspectives*, pp. 18–28. Statistics Canada Catalogue No. 75–001-XPE. 1997; McLanahan, "Parent Absence or Poverty? Which Matters More?", In *Consequences of Growing Up Poor*, Edited by: Duncan, G. J. and Brooks-Gunn, J. 33–48, (New York: Russell Sage Foundation), 1997.

Chapter Four

Prevalence of Institutional Regionalism in Societies

As identities and families, institutions are also fragmented along the lines of a conservative and a liberal identity in a process I termed *institutional regionalism*. Regionalism occurs both within and among institutions. It can occur between institutions positioned in different locales and within institutions - that is, among units and co-workers carrying different identities. Institutional regionalism can have both positive and negative effects, namely, it can create situations of *constructive and destructive competition* among the identity groups. The most striking example of destructive competition is a civil war, whereas global cities are illustrative of a constructive competition, which nurtures societal cohesion and solidarity. Although modern cities are in themselves good examples of internal regionalisms and tension, they are also models for the future global society built on a sustained social integration and mutual support.

It has also generally been the case that spatial proximity inherent to cities alleviates tension, fosters close interaction and cooperation between regionally-defined communities. It creates a situation of constructive competition. It is thus appropriate to assume that spatial proximity alleviates social tension between the distinctive identity groups largely due to the fact that they are positioned in close proximity to one another and perceive that there is much more to gain through cooperation than conflict. One of the main prerequisites for a constructive competition is that either identity in power must adopt a policy of inclusion resulting in a mutual support and common interest within the confines of the political-legal entities they are functioning in, which can be a nation-state, a city, a region of the world, or a province in a country.

Institutional regionalism is manifested in such common forms of clientelism such as nepotism, cronyism, and other forms of patron-client networks which consciously produce discriminatory treatment toward members of a distinct identity group. Such practices are widespread in the system of social services, the consumption sector, educational services, and state institutions across the world. Members of a distinctive identity group are often denied jobs, lodging, or provided low quality services and treatment, thereby generating political and societal contention.

CORRUPTION

Corruption is most commonly described as the abuse of public office for private gain. Modern research has tied the corruption phenomenon to such factors as oversized public sector, poor quality of regulatory institutions, the lack of democratic governance, low wages of public officials, and lack of economic competition.[1]

In this book, I seek to illustrate the process of corruption in the context of the identity relations and identity dualism. From this perspective, corruption is a process of creation of administrative and legalistic barriers by the dominant identity to demote the social status of the minority group. At the same time, it is a means for different identity groups to reconcile divergent interests and to facilitate mutually beneficial solutions. In a similar vein, polities that experience the lack of rule of law and those ruled by authoritarian leaders have high levels of corruption[2] owing to the fact that the ruling identity erects such informal social and administrative barriers in efforts to demote the social status of a rival identity group, which is often forced to purchase services from institutions dominated by another group and to overcome the administrative barriers intentionally imposed for it.

For different identity groups working in the same institution, corruption provides a venue to achieve shared solutions and profits while avoiding a conflict of interest. The corruption phenomenon and its modern interpretation imply an illicit purchase of services, especially with respect to the involvement of state officials in such activities. It implies the abuse of administrative power by officials for private gain. However, there are various types of corruption, such as grand corruption, involving politicians accepting bribes to influence laws, extortive corruption, and collusive corruption. Collusive corruption occurs when the owner of an unqualified project manages to get approval by bribing an official. Extortive corruption occurs when an official demands a bribe to approve qualified projects. The granting of permits and licenses by bureaucrats with near monopoly on power resembles this type of corruption.[3]

However, according to my interpretation, corruption is a process in which various identity groups seek mutually beneficial solutions through the exchange of services. The corruption phenomenon is less prevalent in societies where the level of social harmony is high and that enjoy a high degree of transparency of political processes and governance as opposed to countries plagued by the identity confrontation and the exclusivist nature of regimes.[4] It is, therefore, appropriate to argue that there is no reason for corruption to flourish in countries where there is a high degree of the identity homogeneity, where the need to trespass the legal boundaries arises rarely, if at all. However, there is a high degree of demand for the so called "shadow economy" in countries where the identities establish a pattern of domination and must constantly find ways to reconcile conflicting interests.

As such, there is no demand for corruption in societies build on the principles of social equality and justice, as well as the political transparency. The very meaning of corruption lies in the creation of administrative barriers by the dominant identity towards a rival group in efforts to foster rent farming and to stratify the society in accordance with the identity configurations. Corruption is an illicit acquisition of services from a public official or institution by individuals or institutions that are unable to access them normally. In a situation like that, the entire socio-legal structure is constructed in such a way as to foster extortive corruption by public officials that have the identity bonds, from those supposedly belonging to a different identity group. However, societies that are built on a social consensus where the level of corruption is low construct and enact formal and informal laws that harmonize with the needs of the population at large, which transcend the identity linkages and avert the creation of artificial barriers as opposed to the polities where there is a relatively high contestation for space among the identity groups.

Periods of economic and political transition are often cited as some of the major causes of corruption. Considering the case of post-Soviet Russia is particularly relevant in this context. Viewing it in light of the transition from one identity group to another can provide us with a better understanding of the real reasons behind the corruption phenomenon since those periods witnessed a process of redistribution of resources, powers, properties and assets, when the need to reconcile the divergent interests and avoid a conflict was the highest. In addition, Yong finds that economic transition is one of the main roots of corruption in transitional China.[5] Likewise, post-conflict polities are highly likely to experience the rise of corruption, especially if one identity group takes power after another and the subsequent redistribution of powers and resources. Oftentimes, authoritarian regimes are characterized as being highly corrupt. I find an explanation to that in the fact that in authoritarian polities; corruption is part of the power identity's constructed administrative and socio-cultural barrier which serves the purpose of levying a minority identity. In developed nations, where the level of corruption is low, those identity groups that hold power create conditions for the social harmony through addressing the needs of the wider population.

Le Billon argues that "corruption resulting from the legacies of war economies and a culture of impunity undermines liberal reforms, resulting in suboptimal outcomes." He stresses that

> corruption is institutionalized within peace building and reconstruction initiatives. Although it may not be corruption *stricto sensu*, nepotism, fraud, overinvoicing, lack of transparency and accountability, and tax avoidance have characterized various forms of foreign engagement during the transition process. The risk is that these types of "corruption" undermine the integrity, efficiency, legitimacy and role-modeling of peace building and reconstruction initiatives. [6]

Institutional regionalism is also one of the causes of provoked mobility especially when there is a pronounced trend for the identity group in power to establish or maximize its dominance while neglecting the needs of a distinctive identity group or even facilitating the process of migration whereby minority individuals can coalesce with majorities situated in different locales, which was particularly the case in the Soviet Union where a whole social class of dissidents existed that were subjected to various kinds of social pressures and discrimination, and whose isolation from the overlapping liberal identity was warranted by the existence of the Iron Curtain. With the creation of the Gulag labor camps, the Soviet leadership hoped to first of all suppress the dissent of those estranged from the political and social processes in what was then a new Soviet polity.

A class of political dissidents was a class of social outcasts mainly composed of intellectuals who openly voiced their pro-western liberal worldviews in a nation that had been taken over by the people from the working class who adhered to such principles as conservatism, egalitarianism and equality through the victimization of the formerly privileged social strata. An underprivileged social class during the monarchy, the working class became the moving force of Soviet revolution which was to fill in the leadership positions in new political elite. The czarism era elite were those who benefited from the monarchy in economic terms and who suddenly became targets for reprisals by the newly-formed government. For example, Sheila Fitzpatrick believes that opportunities for social mobility and access to power have been instrumental in legitimizing the regime during the Stalinist period. [7] According to various estimates the number of victims of the so called Great Purge, a series of persecution campaigns conducted under the leadership of Joseph Stalin and Lavrentiy Beria in 1937-38 range from 681,692 to almost 2 million. [8]

Notably, state identities rarely impede people's attempts to migrate because of economic considerations since migrants send their earnings to their families situated in home countries which adds up to a significant share of the national GDP. Expulsion of an alien identity allows the dominant identity to flourish. As the World Bank data suggests, in 2013, China received more than 38 billion US dollars in a form of remittances from its migrants working overseas, India received more than 68 billion in 2012, France received more than 22 billion in 2013, Pakistan - 14 billion, Mexico - 22 billion, Ukraine - almost 10 billion, and the Philippines with more than 26 billion US dollars in remittances.[9] It is important to note that many migrants choose to apply for permanent residency and citizenship in countries of employment as a result of having been better adapted to new environments with a wealth of opportunities for personal realization and social integration.

However, sometimes, identity groups in a pursuit of a territorial dominance resort to a forceful deportation and even mass physical elimination of an adversary group in order to eradicate the barriers to a complete dominance over space. The only explanation for the occurrence of mass deportations and mass killing is that a dominating identity group is no longer willing to tolerate the presence of an alien group within its sphere of influence. One important example which illustrates a sudden shift of the identities is the rise to power of the Nazi regime in Germany and its persecution of various groups of people defined by race, religion, ethnic, and other backgrounds. Persecution of the ethnic Uyghur population in the Xinjiang Autonomous Region of China by the Han majority ethnic group and their coercive assimilation policies toward the Uyghur ethnicity demonstrate how a majority identity represses a minority group as a result of non-alignment concerns.

Another notable instance of the identity non-alignment is a centuries-old hostility between the Russians and the Muslim minority ethnic groups of the Caucasus region of Russia where outbreaks of deadly violence continue to this day. The Russian government has been able to reduce the level of contention from an outright international conflict involving foreign mercenaries and external funding of rebels to sporadic clashes between government forces and Islamic militant groups, and occasional terrorist acts. Current Russian policies of sustaining stability in that highly volatile region largely depend on a significant federal funding rather than on increasing the liberties and access to institutions of power for different groups representing various societal strata and ethnic groups. Only by 2016, Chechnya is expected to receive more than 3.5 billion US dollars in federal funding, which is an enormous amount for the republic with a population of only 1.2 million.[10] State regulation of financial flows and the containment of a civil society sector allowed the center to inhibit secessionism and to consolidate federalism, not only in the Caucasus region but also countrywide. Whereas the Yeltsin-era reforms were geared to reinforce stability through the promotion of liberalism and consensus-making, the Putin-era reforms witnessed a significant reliance on state power institutions, the centralization of executive power and instruments of social coercion in maintaining stability, which is, by and large insufficient and even detrimental for the attempts to build a long-lasting peace.

INSTITUTIONAL REGIONALISM

Regionalism in education and scholarship is a form of institutional regionalism whereby various scientific, educational, and sponsorship institutions representing different locales create mutual support networks based on the identity alignment as well as produce patterns of constructive competition with institutions of the same and, oftentimes, of a distinctive identity group. Institutional regionalism is also prevalent within certain institutions, namely, when members of different identities work in the same private or public institution, creating patterns of either constructive or destructive competition. Destructive competition results in grievances and inter-personal conflicts which can be expressed through a verbal confrontation and even physical violence.

> For most organizations, dispute and disciplinary proceedings are dyadic in nature: An employee may have some dispute with the supervisor; an employee may be subject to disciplinary action by the supervisor. . . . A key to understanding apparent differences in workplace justice outcomes, then, may be the sex composition and nature of the interaction between complainants and those to whom complaints are brought. [11]

In their field observation, Dalton et al. find that grievances were most likely to be resolved in favor of the lower power disputant when the supervisor-employee dyad was comprised of two males. [12] Whereas it is important to account for the gender composition and relative power imbalances among the disputants, as a general rule, an absence of the identity alignment warrants a rejection of employment candidates at the interview level or in the initial phase of employment. In this respect, gender composition among the disputants plays a key role because of differentiating gender roles in sustaining the identities and females' strong attachment to land. Thus, even a male supervisor can make substantial concessions, provide patronage or grant privileges to a female employee in order to maintain some degree of attachment to land. Whereas, as a general rule, males tend to hold supervisory positions, subordinate females often have a great amount of leverage over the decisions made at the level of the institution owing to an inherent attachment to land.

Institutional regionalism is clearly evident in the admission practices of institutions derived from a necessity to sustain the homogeneity of institutional identities by accepting applicants of an aligning identity group. Members of a distinctive identity group are generally denied admission to employment and study opportunities at institutions dominated by one identity which paves the way to the aggravation of institutional regionalism. A notable instance of institutional regionalism and a conflict of interest with the state is when certain private and public institutions run by one identity group establish cooperative networks with foreign companies, or function independently in a state run by a different identity group, which leads to a contestation in the economic, political, legal, and social sphere. The state can seize and appropriate the assets of a company, and arrest its leaders on often fabricated charges since there is a relative power imbalance between state power in the hands of one identity group and private business in other's even in a modern constitutional state like Russia where law can easily become an instrument of manipulation in the hands of the ruling identity group. A good example of such a scenario is the Yukos affair and the arrest of its head Mikhail Khodorkovsky in 2003, who was released in 2014 after spending 10 years in prison only to be expelled from Russia. [13]

Likewise, many firms and private enterprises are revoked their licenses because of grave and uncompromising issues with the governing structures as a result of non-alignment. Using various types of mechanisms, including multiple inspections, extortions, and persecution, they undermine their activity by all means at their disposal. Conversely, companies can often freely transcend the legal or ethical boundaries owing to their identity linkages with the governance institutions - the reason why companies can get nationalized after a shift of the identity groups in power, since the monopolization of the market by the state serves the economic needs of the ruling identity group. Private companies can turn into instruments of economic coercion and power of the dominant identity group following its rise to political power. After another shift of the identities in power the process can be reversed with private companies occupying the vast majority of space on the market and state power being checked and balanced by significant private interests. It is, therefore, appropriate to claim that sometimes there is a clear-cut division line between state power in the hands of one identity group and private sector largely occupied by another group.

Given the situation of destructive competition, contestation between the two identity groups takes form of a violent power struggle between the state and private interest, which is often allied with a civil society sector, while the absence of checks on state power imposed by a civil society renders the distribution of power and benefits among rival identity groups disproportionate and aggravates competition to the point when repressions and unlawful arrests become a norm. A situation of relative power imbalance of such nature forces civil society institutions and the social strata associated with them to transform into underground organizations with only marginal potential to influence state policies. Nevertheless, this is not always the case and the identities can co-exist in the absence of substantial tensions given there is an agreement among groups to retain such a labor division pattern and distribution of powers. It is through both constructive and destructive competition that identity groups promote a policy of territorial dominance. The difference is that in a latter case, it is a form of contestation, while in the former case it is oftentimes a violent struggle.

ALCOHOLISM AND SUICIDE

The problem of alcoholism and drug abuse among many people of the working age is often produced by the inability to achieve personal and professional realization as a result of being "unfit" in a community. For instance, unemployment is cited as one of the major causes of alcoholism[14], among other factors, leading to depression and, sometimes, to suicide. In most cases, however, those unable to find employment in their indigenous locales are compelled to seek a job in different places, which serves as a basis for regionalism. A study by Miller and Millman consider the so called "innocent bystanders" who are not consciously intending to harm the alcoholic.

> Most of the time, there is not conscious intent to help the alcoholic continue the drinking and the suicide. However, there are motives that are not always noble that lurk unconsciously. These frequently arise out of self-defense in the face of alcoholism. The alcoholic is an intimidating beast who can provoke and foster resentments that paralyze those affected by the alcoholic and render them incapable of making rational decisions regarding the welfare of the alcoholic. The resentment is more likely to drive the enabler to drive the enabler to undermine the attempts by the alcoholic to achieve sobriety.[15]

In a similar vein, the problem of suicide has been discussed in the context of social, psychiatric, and psychological problems encountered by the victim. Health problems were also found to be important factors attributed to commitment of suicide, especially among the terminally ill patients. Suicide among adolescents is common and has often been associated with problems related to social integration, family issues, and school problems. Relevant in that context is Emile Durkheim's scale for social integration which placed altruism at the high end and egoism at the low end. Durkheim implied that both high and low levels of social integration cause high suicide rates, while a moderate level causes few.[16] Durkheim assigns the term *anomie* to a state of low regulation.[17] For instance, when society has weak regulation over a person, he or she is relatively free to pursue whether or not and how to commit suicide. *Anomie*, specifically, occurs among businessmen during depressions, as well as among widows, widowers, and divorced people. High levels of state regulation can also be conducive to an increase in suicide rates, which is true in authoritarian nations or those where high social pressures and stern traditions prevail. It is important to highlight Durkheim's finding that suicide rates are higher among men than among women, especially among single men, or people without children. He also found that suicide rates are higher in times of peace, than in time of war. These findings also imply a single male's or person's without children weak connection to land as opposed to married couples and those with children, whereby they are subjected to social forces aimed at expulsion and homogenization for maintaining and maximizing a territorial dominance of the dominant identity groups. This comes in stark contrast to couples with children who rarely commit suicide. The formation of family provides a high degree of social integration and attachment to land for individuals.

Gvion and Apter also found a strong correlation between aggression, impulsivity and suicide in the academic literature.[18] "Current models suggest that aggression and impulsivity may contribute to a summary factor predictive of suicidal behavior in patients with various types of psychiatric diagnoses."[19] They further highlight a finding, important in the context of social problems and setbacks associated with work:

> Reactive aggression has been associated with lowered serotonin-mediated brain activity, interpersonal rejection, and a pattern of emotional disregulation in the context of interpersonal difficulties and other stressful life events, all of which can lead to suicide.[20]

Although impulsivity and suicide were found to be correlated, many acts of suicide are in fact committed after a thorough decision-making process and planning. Gvion and Apter also suggest that an act of suicide is not always impulsive.[21] A person can also be compelled to commit suicide over a prolonged period of time by various forms of social pressures, exclusion, stigma, and lack of adequate support in times of crises. Often, people diagnosed with HIV are subjected to stigmatization and commit suicide as a result of not receiving adequate medical support and various social pressures produced by stigmatization. It is, therefore, not always appropriate to link impulsivity or aggression and suicide. Aggression can sometimes be viewed as a response to harsh social conditions, injustices and poor treatment to which a person can be subjected throughout the span of lifetime. Both aggression and impulsivity can have a strong correlation with a marital status of a person. It is particularly important to look at a suicide from a standpoint of Durkheim's finding concerning the proneness of single persons and those without children to commit suicide as a result of being subjected to stigmatization resulting from such personal circumstances. Rudowicz found that stigmatization is a very salient factor affecting the psychological well-being of Hong Kong single mothers.[22] However, parenting prevents persons from committing suicide and provides a high degree of social integration.

The role of "passive bystanders" has been considered in the context of the genocide during the Second World War, whose "silent consent" led to the extermination of the identity groups by the German government. While it is important to account for the coercion which is prevalent in situations of war and crises, there is always ample room for action by those not being targeted by the government. Wheeler, for instance, considers the "bystander" role of the UN and leading western nations in resolving the situation in Rwanda in 1994 during a civil war and the genocide committed by the dominant Hutu identity group of the Tutsis.[23]

> Having failed to prevent the outbreak of mass killing in Kigali, the UN Security Council was confronted with the decision of whether it should reinforce the UN forces deployed in late 1993 to monitor the ceasefire between the government and the forces of the Tutsi-dominated Rwandan Patriotic Front (RPF).

More to the point, the western governments failed to qualify the extermination of the Tutsis as genocide in the first place which somewhat supports their bystander stance toward the particular case of mass killing. The situation in Rwanda is a typical scenario according to which two identity groups constantly struggle for dominance and build identity bonds, since prior to the Hutu dominance, the Tutsi identity group was at the helm of the state during Belgium's colonial rule. Belgium saw the Hutus as an "inferior race" as opposed to the Tutsis, who were dubbed "superior".

Considering the US and Great Britain as "passive bystanders" might also be appropriate in the context of the Nazi Germany's campaign of exterminating entire ethnic, racial, and religious groups and failure to intervene to stop mass killing by the Allies, despite being aware of such atrocities. There is a considerable debate on whether or not to draw a clear distinction line between the roles of bystanders and perpetrators, especially in regards to the commitment of crimes against humanity and participation in mass killing. One can be considered complicit on the grounds of absence of acts of resistance to the commitment of a crime, which may or may not qualify as provision of moral support to the perpetrator. Viewing it in light of the identity alignments can improve our understanding of why some people choose to enter into violent conflicts on either side while others simply refrain from doing so, which may not necessarily imply a position of neutrality. In fact, according to my explanation of conflict, the position of neutrality is non-existent because of the identity duality.

For if a person belongs to a liberal identity and resides in a country run by a conservative identity, which instigates an international conflict, that does not qualify him as being neutral or conservative, even if he is conscripted to participate in combat on the government side or otherwise works to support the state regime. In particular, this explains why some parts of the civilian populations tend to support the occupational forces during foreign invasions while others side with the government forces. A person of a liberal identity can also function in or work for the regime or institution run by a conservative identity on the grounds on having special talents or expertise, which is however insufficient to qualify him or her as a person of a conservative identity. In fact, this explains the prevalence and persistence of institutional fragmentation and institutional regionalism when a liberal identity is coerced into working for the regime of a conservative identity which is particularly the case in countries ruled by authoritarian regimes. It also gives rise to underground or outlawed movements whose aim is to disrupt the status quo and bring about a greater degree of social justice.

Considering the role of "passive bystanders" is important in that it highlights problems related to non-alignment of identity groups, fragmented families, and family or spousal regionalism. It is often because of non-alignment concerns in the family that the problem of substance abuse arises, involving both spouses and children. Children and adolescents are particularly prone to being traumatized as a result of the various effects of spousal regionalism, including separation, addiction to drugs, involvement in illicit activities, mental disorders, health problems resulting from mental stress, and commitment of violent acts. Regionalism among siblings is an extension of parental regionalism and is another salient aspect of fragmented families involving favoritism on the part of the parent toward any of the siblings. It generates various forms of competition and resentment among siblings. For instance, Harris and Howard in their study of 600 male and female high school students found that girls more often than boys were perceptive of parental favoritism.[24] The fact that girls were more often perceptive of parental favoritism indicates females' significance in safeguarding the identities and their strong attachment to land.

> The youngest child in the family was more often the favorite of the mother and the middle child was least often a parental favorite. Parental favoritism was associated with perceived parental incompatibility. Teenagers who perceived a sibling as being favored evidenced increased angry and depressive feelings as well as identity confusion. This latter effect was most pronounced when a parent of the same sex favored a sibling of the same sex as the respondent.[25]

Family violence can also exemplify identity non-alignment. It is demonstrative that violence and conflicts within families occur among siblings and spouses. Identity non-alignment among siblings is a very common phenomenon, which explains instances of resentment and violence among siblings, favoritism by the parents, and separation from nuclear families of their members. Though institutional regionalism cannot be always perceived as an outright negative phenomenon, it is not always possible for identities to materialize a constructive competition scenario because of various considerations that can come into play. Destructive competition always has the potential to come about. However, there is a limited trend for distinct identities that work in the same institution to minimize the existing social barriers in efforts to create better working conditions, improve the economic returns, societal cohesion, and to promote self-inclusion in a wider community. Over time, space proximity generates situations of constructive competition and gradually eliminates barriers to a cross-cultural understanding and support. A good example of that is a modern cosmopolitan city which aggregates distinct identity groups around a common economic core into a commune of discrete and yet socially integrated units that carry a wide variety of cultural identities.

Many persistent conflicts among colleagues working in the same environment lead to grave outcomes such as consistent quarrels involving violence while resignations are very often produced by non-alignment issues, rather than random factors. Since it is challenging to identify from the onset of the working process any inconsistencies in the identity alignment, conflicts involving a professional sphere are very common as are their adverse consequences. They include, but are not limited to, psychological traumas, substance abuse, family problems, financial problems, and involvement in illicit activities. For instance, staff members can build alliances with people of the same identity in order to protect and advance common interests, increase shared profits, often at the expense of another identity's interests. Members of distinctive identities working in the same institution can create bonds with people of the same identity extending both within and beyond the confines of the institution, which leads to institutional fragmentation if another identity group comes into conflict and can further result in institutional collapse. The ultimate reason why identities coalesce and institutions fragment lies in the identities' need to expand presence and to suppress the influence of an alien identity group.

Working teams can fragment due to the incompatibility of identities which jeopardizes common interests embodied in institutional goals, which is why much emphasis is made on the selection of candidates not only with sufficient skills and expertise but also with a proper identity alignment. This formed the basis of a policy of selection of operatives and agents in the security apparatus of the Soviet Union. Being able to distinguish between a liberal and a conservative identity is a crucial skill among recruiters in the intelligence institutions as a whole. The main objective of intelligence and military institutions is to protect the integrity and dominance of the identity groups in power, and to preserve the existing identity configuration according to which they can hold the leadership position. Recruitment based on the identity alignment was part of the so called Ideological department in the Communist Party of the Soviet Union. It was generally staffed by people experienced in the occupation and, what is more important, very sensitive to even slight deviations in political, ideological, and identity orientations. They often were key figures behind the process of selection of individuals for political persecution and removal of individuals from leading political and administrative positions.

NOTES

1. Mishra, Ajit. *Corruption*, (Princeton: Princeton University Press), 2009, Source: http://search.proquest.com.libraryproxy.griffith.edu.au/docview/189251340?accountid=14543 (accessed August 11, 2014).

2. Based on the Transparency International's 2011 Bribe Payers Survey of business people from the 28 countries and territories in the Bribe Payers Index, the Netherlands and Switzerland top the list with scores of 8.8, with Belgium, Germany and Japan following closely behind. Companies from these countries are seen as less likely to engage in bribery than the other countries ranked. At the end of the list, companies from China and Russia are perceived to be most likely to engage in bribery abroad. The business people surveyed perceived bribery by companies from these countries to be most widespread, resulting in much lower scores for China and Russia than the other surveyed countries.

3. Mishra, Ajit. *Corruption*, (Princeton: Princeton University Press), 2009, Source: http://search.proquest.com.libraryproxy.griffith.edu.au/docview/189251340?accountid=14543 (accessed August 11, 2014).

4. Consider, for instance, the developed countries of the West, and in particular, the countries of Scandinavia where the corruption index is among the lowest in the world. Countries of Asia are often characterized as being corrupt owing to particular cultural features of their societies. For instance, bribery is considered an integral part of the Eurasian societies, such as Russia and the countries of Central Asia, which supports a system of rent-farming deeply embedded in the state.

5. Yong, Guo. "How does Economic Transition Breed Corruption?", *China Economic Journal*, Vol. 1, Iss. 2, 2008.

6. Le Billon, Philippe. "Corrupting Peace? Peace-building and Post-conflict Corruption," *International Peacekeeping*, Vol. 15, Is. 3, 2008, p. 345.

7. Fitzpatrick, Sheila. "Stalin and the Making of a New Elite, 1928–1939", *Slavic Review*, Vol. 38, Iss. 3, 1979, p. 38, pp. 377-402.

8. Pipes, Richard. *Communism: A History*, (Modern Library Chronicles), 2001, p. 67.

9. World Bank staff estimates based on IMF balance of payments data, Source: http://data.worldbank.org/indicator/BX.TRF.PWKR.CD.DT.

10. "Russian Investments to Chechnya will be 128 billion Rubles by 2016", 2014, Source: http://www.pravda.ru/news/districts/south/groznyi/08-04-2014/1203676-invest-0/.

11. Dalton, D. R., Todor, W. D. & Owen, C. L. "Workplace Justice Outcomes as a Function of Adversaries' Gender Composition: A Field Assessment", *Journal of Business and Psychology*, 1, 1987, pp. 203-217.

12. Ibid.

13. Khodorkovsky arrives in Germany after release from prison, *The Guardian*, 21 December 2013, Source: http://www.theguardian.com/world/2013/dec/20/mikhail-khodorkovsky-germany-prison-pardon-putin (Accessed 6 August, 2014).

14. Other factors are considered in many studies as well, including a genetic predisposition, psychological, psychiatric, and morality disorders, social, and financial problems.

15. Miller, Norman and Millman, Robert. "A Common Cause of Alcoholism," *Journal of Substance Abuse Treatment*, Volume 6, Issue 1, 1989, Pages 41-43.

16. Durkheim, Emile. *Suicide: A Study in Sociology*, Book 2, Chapter 5, pp. 246-254, 258, (The Free Press), 1897. Durkheim asserted that egoism is a far more common cause of high suicide rates in modern societies than is *anomie*.

17. Ibid., pp. 356-358.

18. Gvion, Yari and Apter, Alan. "Aggression, Impulsivity, and Suicide Behavior: A Review of the Literature," *Archives of Suicide Research*, Vol. 15, Iss. 2, 2011, pp. 93-112.

19. Ibid., p. 95.

20. Ibid., p. 95.

21. Ibid., p. 98.

22. Rudowicz, Elisabeth. "Stigmatization as a Predictor of Psychological Well-being of Hong Kong Single Mothers," *Marriage and Family Review*, Vol. 33, Iss. 4, 2001, p. 63.

23. Wheeler, Nicholas. Global Bystander to Genocide: International Society and the Rwandan Genocide of 1994. In: Saving Strangers: Humanitarian Intervention in International Society, Oxford University Press, 2002, http://www.oxfordscholarship.com/view/10.1093/0199253102.001.0001/acprof-9780199253104-chapter-8, (Accessed August 15, 2014).

24. Harris, Irving and Howard, Kenneth. Correlates of Perceived Parental Favoritism, *The Journal of Genetic Psychology*, Vol. 146, Iss.1, 1985.

25. Ibid.

Chapter Five

Concluding Remarks

IDENTITY EQUILIBRIUM

A path to global peace lies in a necessity to maintain the equilibrium of the identities. It implies the creation of conditions for social equality and harmony, open access to opportunities for social realization, elimination of administrative and social barriers for the identity group to flourish, including increasing the transparency of political and electoral processes, maximization and improvement of instruments of social control over the decision- and policy-making processes, elimination of concealed discrimination, stigmatization, and exclusionary policies discussed earlier in the book.

SPATIAL PROXIMITY AS A MEANS OF AMELIORATING CONFLICT

Spatial proximity has generally assisted in initiating a process of reconciliation among warring parties, of which there are multiple examples. Oftentimes, it is only until after the negotiators come to the negotiation table that a full-fledged reconciliation process commences among warring parties. Spatial proximity creates conditions for the contestants to voice their concerns and fears and hear those of their opponents' firsthand. This allows them to find mutually-beneficial solutions and to conclude a violent conflict.

While it is important to account for the point in a protracted violent conflict at which the belligerents come to understand the futility of warfare, the meeting between the leaders of the warring parties often marks the beginning point of the reconciliation.

It is thus appropriate to assume that physical proximity is an important factor in the process of reconciliation. For instance, Jones conducted a study of 441 patients in 10 intermediate-care nursing homes and observed the significance of both closeness and distance for the maintenance of friendships among patients of the nursing home.[1] Another study conducted by Fay and Maner found a fundamental link between physical warmth and social affiliation.[2] Findings from the two experiments support their hypothesis that physical warmth serves as a symbolic cue signaling the close proximity of a source of affiliation. It is an important finding for improving the understanding of how large-scale conflicts can be resolved through physical contact between the belligerents. Conversely, distances produce animosities.

It is spatial or regional proximity which creates a perception among neighboring countries of closeness and collective vulnerability relative to those situated farther away. The closer the countries are situated to one another the lower the chance of them having substantial and long-term disputes and combat situations. Over time, physical proximity can provide opportunities to make concessions by any of the belligerent parties and to begin the process of conflict transformation whereby issues can be resolved by non-violent means, that is, through the dialogue and consensus.

NOTES

1. Jones, Dean. "Spatial Proximity, Interpersonal Conflict, and Friendship Formation in the Intermediate-Care Facility", *The Gerontologist*, 1975, Volume 15, pp. 150-154.

2. Fay, Adam and Maner, Jon. "Warmth, Spatial Proximity, and Social Attachment: The Embodied Perception of a Social Metaphor", *Journal of Experimental Social Psychology*, 2012, Volume 48, Issue 6, pp. 1369-1372.

Part 2

Chapter Six

Identity Duality and International Relations

MOVING BEYOND THE ANARCHY MODE

Whereas scholars of classical realism stress that human nature and human drive for power to be the main factors of influence in the global political structure, neorealists argue that states largely pursue relative gains and security objectives in an anarchical global environment. Neoliberal institutionalists maintain that states pursue absolute gains and that they are the main actors which create institutions transcending national divides to more effectively pursue power and, more importantly, wealth. Neoliberalism particularly stresses the importance of interdependence which is "a solvent of conflict and a creator of cooperation."[1] Whereas neoliberals significantly underscore the role of domestic processes in shaping the structure of international system, neorealists are critical of such "reductionist" explanations of the system.[2]

The proponents of social constructivism stress the role of shared ideas, norms, and interests behind a neorealist and neoliberal overwhelmingly materialist foundation of structure.[3] "The dominant approach in mainstream political science is to treat ideas in causal terms as a typically (intervening variable) that explain some proportion of behavior beyond the effects of power, interest, and institutions alone."[4] Thus, for instance, neoliberals do not reject the ideational component of processes, yet only "to the extent that they have effects beyond effects of power, interest, and institutions."[5]

> The constitutive debate between materialists and idealists is not about the relative contribution of ideas versus power and interest to social life. The debate is about the relative contribution of brute material forces to power and

63

interest explanations. Materialists cannot claim power and interest as "their" variables; it all depends on how the latter are constituted. [6]

Wendt defines "brutes material forces" as "things which exist and have certain causal powers independent of ideas, like human nature, the physical environment, and, perhaps, technological artifacts."[7] He suggests that "material capabilities do have some intrinsic causal powers."[8]

> It is the relationship of these [material capabilities] to interests (and shared ideas or culture) that determine the quality of international life. [9]

The main problem underlying the classical realism's approach to international affairs is that current understanding of state interest, "relative gain", or as classical realists would put it "interest defined in terms of power,"[10] and private interest as such, is confined to a pursuit of power by actors, whether individuals, social groups, or states. From that perspective, states are aggressive and opportunistic actors which are principally driven by self-interest, defined in terms of power. Neorealism argues that states are rather more cautious than aggressive actors driven by the personal security concerns.

Neoliberal institutionalism does not differ extensively from both classical realism and neorealism in that states still pursue self-interest, which is defined in terms of "absolute gain" and economic power, pursued by means of institutionalized cooperation, reciprocal adjustment and due to interdependence among the discreet units in a global system. However, Keohane recognizes the limitations of approaching the question of 'how the structure is constituted' from the standpoint of power and wealth.

> . . . the concepts of power and wealth have a common deficiency as the basis for explanations of behavior: to estimate the power of actors, or whether a given product, service, or raw material constitutes wealth, one has to observe behavior—in power relationships or in markets."[11]

Keohane's views do not substantially diverge from or advance a neorealist stance with respect to power and wealth and are rather meant to supplement them. Specifically, for neoliberal institutionalists, states significantly focus on maximizing their power and wealth, albeit by forming transnational institutions and regimes encompassing various states and divergent interests which in some way or another converge in a common purpose. For neoliberals, cooperation means "mutual adjustment."[12] They significantly rely on domestic politics and state structures in their conceptualization of international politics and on the role played by institutions in forging common policies which transcend the national divides, whereas realists, such as Morghenthau, define power as "man's control over the minds and actions of other men."[13]

Nye, in turn, stresses the role of what he calls "soft power"- that is, the use of incentives, rather than force, to influence other actors' behavior, which also explains why states create institutions encompassing a diversity of interests and levels of power. Nye defined soft power as "getting others to want the outcomes that you want", "it [soft power] co-ops people rather than coerces them."[14] In comparing the soft power use on an international scale with interpersonal relations, Nye suggests that ". . . power does not necessarily reside with the larger partner, but in the mysterious chemistry of attraction."[15] Soft power lies in the ability ". . . to attract and persuade".[16]

> The ability to establish preferences tends to be associated with intangible assets such as an attractive personality, culture, political values and institutions, and policies that are seen as legitimate or having moral authority. If a leader represents values that others want to follow, it will cost less to lead.[17]

Nye differentiates between coercive power and payments - that is, sticks and carrots, on the one hand, and the ability to attract, on the other.[18] However, he does not explain the underlying divergence of key values among actors at all levels of the system which produces an incongruence of behavior and, thereby, a conflict—a situation in which soft power use is ineffective and sometimes even detrimental. In the absence of trust between the contentious parties, much of which derives from the alignment of the identity groups, setting an example for others to follow or attempting to persuade an adversary to follow suit can lead to extremely aggravating consequences as it inevitably impinges on the indigenous values and principles of actors. In particular, freedom is the most fundamental value which is deeply embedded in all cultures and traditions across the world. Yet, cultures quite often tend to collide because of the underlying divergence in understandings and expressions of freedom among the distinctive agents and social groups which explains the occurrence of conflict on a wider scale. While important in its own right, soft power use is futile and ineffective in the absence of trust and in situations where there is an underlying divergence of key values and identities among state actors.

Thus, even if we assume that distinctive actors can in rare cases come to terms with respect to a common pursuit of certain goals within the framework of an institution, there is often a high degree of a suspicious attitude prevalent among stakeholders which undermines common effort and renders such institutions ineffective. The efficacy of the United Nation's Security Council has been significantly undermined by the divergent interests, and, more importantly, values, among its core constituent members. With the accession of Russia to the World Trade Organization in 2012, its trade relations with the countries of the West have barely experienced any progress even since the fall of the communism raising significant doubts about the effectiveness of its membership for the domestic economic growth. Political tensions between Russia and the West over the crisis in Ukraine have further exacerbated Russia's trade relations with the West.

Although the two main schools of thought in international relations differ, both are most commonly seen as largely based on rationalism with neoliberals essentially complementing a neorealist approach. The two main schools vary in their explanation of the effects of the anarchy on international relations.[19] Namely, neorealists believe that there always exists a threat of conflict with other states which leads them to make utilitarian and security-oriented adjustments to their policies in relation to other actors owing to an anarchical nature of the international system. According to both neorealists and neoliberals actions of actors are rendered predictable to a certain level by the intricate interplay between state interest, policies, and, more importantly, ways of advancing those policies on an international level. From a neorealist perspective, states seek security, but not necessarily by means of coercive hegemonic power (which would be the case for the offensive neorealists) that can be projected on other states. Rather, states strive to build a sound foundation for their long-term security through forging of interest-based alliances which makes a neorealist approach significantly resemble a neoliberal emphasis on the construction of transnational institutions as a path to more effectively reach one's ends.

States constantly seek deterrence through the balance of powers in their relations with other states, yet only in light of the perception of threat to their security and national integrity since the balance of powers represents a belligerent aspect in inter-state relations and often reflects a high level of suspicious attitude, which inevitably produces reciprocity. It also reflects either a tacit or explicit hostility among state actors. Otherwise, states simply do not randomly pursue a policy of deterrence through the balance of powers with respect to other states but rather strive to rely on cooperative behavior and a convergence of interest in forging common goals predominantly with overlapping regimes. They strive to form coalitions only with countries that are not seen as posing any real or potential threat which corresponds to the argument made by the democratic peace theory. In particular, states most often avoid building coalitions with politically or ideologically unaligned actors.

States always strive to accumulate a deterrent potential only in light of being threatened, both explicitly and tacitly, by the policies and interests of another state—an attitude that can change over time as one state regime is always succeeded by another which may espouse a distinctive approach to foreign relations. In this respect, Walt develops a theory of the "balance of threats" which addresses the issue of the counterpoising threats as the main vehicle of the coalition formation among state actors.[20]

However, most scholars, including Walt, see "ideological and cultural similarities" to be most responsible for the creation of alliances between polities which is erroneous since they can merely manifest an underlying similarity of an innate identity. Walt maintains that states entering an alliance can either "balance" or "bandwagon": i.e., ally against or alongside a state which is a principal source of threat.[21] The former represents a more common scenario, while the latter is an example of a notorious Soviet-German non-aggression pact. It is also unclear how one can differentiate between the accumulation of threat and power since the underlying criteria and purpose of state power lie in its demonstrative effect on relations with other states which, by and large, equates to a demonstration of threat vis-à-vis other actors, whether real or potential adversaries. I do not believe that states seek to demonstrate a threat or power to nations that are aligned to them in terms of their political and socio-cultural worldviews but only do so toward their competitors on an international political arena. This serves as the main motivation factor for the creation of coalitions among polities.

Continuity of policies vis-à-vis the external actors in large part depends on a proximity of state regimes, e.g., how closely ruling regimes can be aligned in terms of their political affiliation and other explicit identity features, such as the religious affiliation, ethnicity, and position in an international economic hierarchy. Yet, what really lies behind those alignments could be a belonging to a certain identity group in which most commonly known forms of social association tend to resemble. Those can be a shared religious background, political views, or ethno-cultural links. States never seek deterrence in relations with closely aligned actors—that is, other states with converging political and socio-cultural worldviews. Cases of alignment among state identities almost always preclude the possibility of an outright military conflict.

Thus, one needs to question the conception that states are strictly autonomous actors driven by the individualistic pursuits and rational-egoistic assumptions as well as a belief that state policies are driven by the "shared ideational aspects" as they can merely manifest an overarching congruence of inherent identity groups. It also reflects a highly fluid nature of state borders which fits well into Katzenstein's description of "porous regions" and is also aligned with the general argument made by social constructivists, such as Adler and Barnett about the role of "security communities".[22] They borrowed the term from Deutsch who originally saw them as "a group of people who believe that they have come to agreement on at least this one point: that common social problems must and can be resolved by processes of peaceful change".[23]

Deutsch defines peaceful change as "the resolution of social problems, normally by institutionalized procedures, without resort to large-scale physical force."[24] Adler and Barnett, in turn, modified the definition of security communities as having shared identities, values, and interests. However, defining communities in terms of both a pursuit of collective security and shared identities is likewise insufficient as it does not account for the prevailing wide political and social contentiousness which overrides all kinds of common purpose that might supposedly exist within certain regional communities as well as a highly transparent and fluid nature of legal and physical boundaries of various political entities, of which states and regions are one kind.

Defining distinctive population groups as cohesive communities destined to pursue a common purpose defined as security is erroneous as it does not conform to the overriding reality which exists within states and international institutions encompassing a number of states, broad and highly entrenched political and social tensions among the distinctive identity groups, namely, their struggle for power and resources both within a state and global system. In addition to that, that definition does not account for the overwhelming significance of migration flows in a global political and economic system which transcend the legal and physical boundaries of all forms of political entities.

In this regard, Katzenstein rightly described regions as having a porous nature. For instance, much depends on a nature of leadership and elite groups in any given nation which advance the interests of a specific social strata and appropriate identity groups which represent their target constituencies. Those elite groups sustain transnational bonds which ultimately build into a global network of likeminded individuals that form collectivities of aligned identity groups that embody common interest and purpose.

Neoliberals are similarly concerned about states' pursuit of power and wealth, but rather as a "means of want satisfaction" against the backdrop of the anarchical world system of which they are an integral part. They also stress a lack of information about the intentions and genuine goals of actors in "reaching and keeping agreements even where common interests for cooperation exist" which compels states to create transnational regimes in order to make the behavior of state actors more predictable. [25]

Thus, both schools make their arguments against the backdrop of the anarchical global society in which states pursue their ego-centric objectives, defined as wealth and power. Whereas neorealists contend that states are primarily concerned about their security in a highly competitive and hierarchical world system where weak states tend to hold underprivileged positions relative to strong states even though in a legal sense they might be entirely equal. In reality, however, weak states are equipped with minimal capacities to influence the global processes, the reason why liberals contend that states aspire to create transnational institutions with great powers in an effort to maximize their own returns and influence through the symbiotic relationship, defined in terms of a common pursuit of wealth, as a "means of want satisfaction" and "economic power" which simultaneously equips them with the military preponderance.

However, it is important to note that minor states do not enter alliances randomly with any and all global powers but do so selectively, only with appropriate actors that are assessed on the basis of their alignment in terms of their mainstream political and socio-cultural orientation, much of which derives from which particular identity group or elite group holds power in any given group of polities and to what extent these groups converge in political and socio-cultural terms. This explains why states often tend to withdraw from certain cooperative agreements in a wake of shifting interests. On the other hand, constructivists are right in that they argue that " . . . states are self-organizing entities whose internal structures confer capacities for institutionalized collective action—corporate agency—on their members."[26]

ON THE PROBLEM OF DOUBLE STANDARDS

Having made a significant reliance on the ideational explanation of processes, constructivists, such as Wendt, have a positivist epistemology of international relations according to which the formation of knowledge can only be based on empiricism and that there cannot be any preconceived linkage between a researcher and the "truth", which is contrary to post-positivism which claims that social science does not grant us privileged access to reality.[27] Here lies a question of what constitutes the "truth" and "objectivity" and a problem of double standards generally arises producing at times irreconcilable differences. Thus, conflicts can only be viewed from the standpoint of "confronting truths" and divergent modes of objectivity as each party always defends its own "particularistic truth" embedded in certain explicit forms, such as a political identity, indigenous customs, or worldviews. Conflicts always tend to erupt as a result of confronting political ideologies which represent a form of truth exhibited by distinctive social units which are produced by their differential perceptions and understandings of most critical ideals, including human liberty and an ideal social organization.

Wendt believes that ". . . international structure consists fundamentally in shared knowledge, and that this affects not only state behavior, but state identities and interests as well."[28] Although not rejecting a neorealist and neoliberal primary concern about the material aspects of power, constructivists essentially play down their role in shaping the structure of political system. For example, Wendt suggests that "material capabilities do have some causal powers."[29] Relevant in this context is a controversy between a descriptive theory of empiricism and a relational theory of postmodernism in that the former relates to "sense-data in the mind" whereas the latter emphasizes "relations among words."[30]

What they are principally concerned is the relationship between the material power and interests embodied in shared ideas and culture."[31] It is in the interaction between the material and ideational aspects that we must look for the ontological essence of international structure. Waltz tries to fill in the rational actors, such as states, with certain motivations which pursue security. It is commonly related to a drive for power.[32] However, I believe that in many cases it is challenging to distinguish between a pursuit of security and power, since one can always imply the other.

Since interest and power are intertwined, behind the variation of interests always lie differential positions of power, which often, albeit not always, produces a conflict. It is in that context that the role of transnational institutions and regimes, whose proponents are neoliberal institutionalists, comes into play as states are similarly interested in a non-violent resolution of a conflict of interest since rarely can a state actor be fully confident in a victory over the adversary in case of launching a war of aggression. Therefore, sometimes, even adversary polities can found a temporary alliance in an effort to prolong the status quo and to gain a better understanding of the adversary's first-strike potential, or to investigate the willingness and potential to cooperate. More importantly, state actors can simply investigate the possibility of promoting overlapping political regimes in different countries by what could be seen as a quest for common ground. That is in line with the classical realism thinking, and particularly, E.H. Carr who advocated temporary agreements of such nature. However, one cannot exclude the possibility that with the creation of alliances between the contentious parties one can always transform hostility into cooperation, namely, when a sudden shift of attitude and focus occurs with respect to dealing with the contentious issues related to domestic and foreign policy which may or may not ensue a non-violent resolution of disputes.

Much depends on reciprocal expectations of actors as well as their perceptions of what their goals are and how they envision their realization in relation to those of other actors. Additionally, another important factor behind actors' policies derives from their prevailing perceptions of how their goals can be realized most effectively. It is largely a matter of the "indigenous" understanding among the distinctive social groups which hold power in polities about how to materialize their most critical objectives vis-à-vis other actors, and whether or not they are determined to pursue a violent way of attaining their goals. Aside from questions of relative power imbalance among key state actors or possible distribution of profits, one needs to ask: what is it that compels states to pursue their goals one way or another or how they create and sustain alliances for the realization of their ends? Utilitarianism explains it in terms of the rational pursuits of actors. However, as I will further elaborate there are differential ways of interpreting and implementing a rational content, which thereby produces a conflict of interest by the distinctive agents and groups espousing various modes of rationality.

Yet, it is still not clear why in some cases states opt for a military confrontation with other states while in others they prefer a peaceful resolution of a conflict of interest. For instance, Van Evera argues that it is the "windows of opportunity" that we must look for the aggressive nature of state foreign policy.[33] Generally speaking, neorealists tend to explain a contradictory nature of state behavior in terms of a pursuit of security, whereby they can achieve their ends by either defensive or offensive means - that is, through the balance of powers or hegemony. I believe, it is important to focus on the patterns of the power struggle in polities and the distribution of political capacities within a state system in order to gain a better understanding of what constitutes the social structure of global order and international affairs.

In addition, Van Evera addresses the issue of the offense-defense overlap, that is, when states pursue offensive ways in politics primarily in order to tackle their security and thereby defensive concerns. In a similar vein, states always pursue security yet they can likewise be perceived by others as having hegemonic aspirations as a result of the uncertainty prevalent in the relations among state actors. In addition, actors are seen as pursuing hegemony only toward what I would call *immediate adversaries*, not remote adversaries, much less allies, which resonates with Wallerstein's approach to world system and the hierarchical nature of global society with the core and peripheral states carrying out their respective functions.[34]

Thus, one state's pursuit of power on an international scale always implies a pursuit of security on the domestic level. In particular, some of the most appalling human experiences in history have been closely associated with a drive by polities to achieve a certain level of security, or to provide welfare to certain population groups under the guise of pursuing the security objectives, which was particularly the case during the two world wars. For instance, contrary to classical realists such as E.H. Carr or Hans Morghenthau, neorealists such as Kenneth Waltz reject any social and idealist aspects behind structural processes.[35] On the other hand, Carr suggests that appeasement is a rationally sound alternative to belligerent politics for one state's realization of goals, which partially resembles a neoliberal approach which actively invokes bargaining techniques in the context of interaction within institutions and regimes.[36]

As an example of such a policy of appeasement, E.H. Carr presents the Soviet-German Non-Aggression Pact and the occupation of Poland in 1939 whereby both parties preferred making concessions in the face of the growing reciprocal military threats. Thus, even if we exclude the possibility of perception of vulnerability by either party, by signing the Pact both nations attempted to widen their time constraints in an effort to better prepare themselves for the upcoming and inevitable warfare.

From a rationalist standpoint on which classical realists as well as neorealists rely so extensively, the Pact was clearly justifiable by the immediate concerns of states. For rationalists, it is reasonable to accept such treaties with hostile regimes even if it can potentially lead to a significant amount of collateral damage in terms of the loss of human life produced by such utterly rationalist ways of thinking and acting. Such a strategy also conforms to the offense-defense theory in that by means of offensive foreign policies and military doctrines states primarily aim to address their foremost security concerns and thereby ensure a higher level of immunity from external threats, to widen the scope of opportunities for political maneuvering that would be available to them in the future. Thus, one way of materializing a strictly rationalist concept in a political realm is by allowing states to resort to belligerent politics and preventive attacks, whose definition can be described as highly fluid, in relations with other actors in an effort to guarantee a higher level of security for their populations.

As appeasement, institutional bargaining, whose proponents are neoliberals, also invokes concessions by parties in order to reach a certain level of trust and to meet the expectations of political actors and to achieve a situation of a functional transparency in a process of interaction whereby the sum of interest produces higher returns. There does not seem to be a significant difference between appeasement and bargaining as both involve concessions and both are ultimately motivated by ego-centric assumptions of stakeholders. The main distinction between the two main rationalist approaches is in that neorealists underscore actors' pursuit of power whereas neoliberals are primarily concerned about the economic interests of state policies in creating common institutions. But how does constructivism explain actors' alignment in a political realm or actors' concessions in the face of the growing hostility exclusively by referring to converging ideological concepts as well as state identities and shared political pursuits?

In addition, it is not always necessary for the weaker party to pursue a policy of appeasement vis-à-vis a stronger state, since all parties to an agreement of which an institution is certainly one kind are bound by shared norms and regulations to act appropriately which renders them equal legalistically to a certain level which resonates with the English School's theorizing in terms of international society bound by public norms.

Essentially, constructivists are concerned about the causal effects of immaterial aspects, such as interests, shared perceptions, preferences, and ideas on material structures and objects. Most importantly, they equate interests and ideas since behind interests there are always ideas. Thus, different ideas dictate various interests which explains a conflict of interest in certain situations, behind which there is always a conflict of ideas. They also underscore that objects are "relationally constructed", rather than "rationally driven" and do not reject a positivist epistemology. In this context, all main schools of thought in international relations can be considered as supportive of positivism. Wendt is right in differentiating between what most neorealists and, particularly, Waltz, and idealists rely on in their conceptualization of "how power is constituted", namely, by "brute material force", on one hand, and "ideas and cultural contexts," on the other.[37] Even classical realists did not reject any social conceptualizations of structure as neorealists do, which is misleading since it limits the scope of the approach to conceptualizing a social structure which must combine both materialistic and ideational aspects.

At the same time, neorealists do not reject the importance of ideology and cultural contexts in driving social and political phenomena. It would be more appropriate to argue for various proportions of materialistic and ideational aspects in constructing the social kind, rather than rejecting a social conceptualization outright. In addition to that, neorealists do not provide a significant substantiation to their rejection of social aspects in driving political phenomena.

RATIONAL INCOMPATIBILITIES

It is not clear what the difference is between what realists conceive as "rationally driven behavior" and a constructivist emphasis on the "ideational aspects". That is, constructivism attempts to explain the materialistic phenomena using the "ideational" tools and to disclose a "contribution of mind and language" which is anchored to external reality.[38] For instance, political realism envisions rationality as a core of both the political processes and the explanatory means aimed to disclose their meaning.

> political realism maintains not only that theory must focus upon rational elements of political reality but also that foreign policy ought to be rational in view of its own moral and practical purposes.[39]

Thus, by focusing on rational elements, theory in turn becomes embedded in rationalism which can be viewed by some as further separating it from the ideational element of structure, which, in fact is not the case. Since rationalism represents a distinctive ideational form it further retains the idealism which is inherent to it.

On the other hand, the meaning of rationality and "rationally driven behavior", to which realists and neoliberals apply their concepts, has not been afforded close attention. In particular, it is unclear what particular goals a rationally driven actor pursues within an international structure. One could argue that rationality is not a constant but a variable subject to a structural change which it ultimately produces. Thus what comes first, rationality or structure? That question constitutes the foundation of the debate between individualism and holism (structuralism). In addition, how can one deprive rationality of the ideational content?

One can always look at rationality from the standpoint of what constitutes a rational form since behind all rational conceptualizations always lies a broad ideational element which ultimately builds into a distinctive social form. Thus, constructivists are right in that they stress the role of ideas, identities, constructed social patterns, and, finally, ideologically-driven conflicts. However, it is not clear how constructivists explain actors' pursuit of goals beyond what realists conceive as the utilitarian thinking. The significance of interaction and ideas from which constructivism derives its core meaning is important for both realists and neorealists as they likewise rely on certain assumptions and ideas which are primarily rooted in what is commonly known as "pragmatic" ways of thinking and acting, rather than a purely "idealistic behavior" associated with the constructivism, of which, it is certainly one kind. In other words, idealism and rationalism cannot be conceived as having entirely separate conceptualizations, since rationalism is driven by ideas whereas all ideas pursue a rational purpose. Since all ideas have a utilitarian purpose they can all be considered as rational. For example, political ideas are always targeted at a certain result which can vary, but most commonly defined in terms of power or access to control over space and resources.

Nevertheless, constructivism does not completely reject rationalism in so far as it can be incorporated in the ideational forms. In other words, rationalism must be looked at as a distinctive way of envisioning the ideational framework, but by no means as separate from it.

That is to say, rationalism is likewise deeply embedded in the ideational framework since all types of rational thinking and acting are driven by certain ideas and cultural contexts of various kinds. Rationalism is just a distinctive form of idealism rooted in materialistic pursuits and ends. It also represents an alternative way of conceptualizing the ideational framework and a different way of expressing an ideology. Thus, presenting constructivism, on the one hand, and realism alongside neorealism, on the other as having irreconcilable epistemological and paradigmatic positions as well as teleological explanations is quite erroneous. All ideational forms ultimately focus on the rational criteria. Any inconsistencies and the "ideological gap" between the rationalist and ideational constructs can be explained by the divergent perceptions and materialization of a rational form by the distinctive groups. Rather, realism represents a distinctive ontological category filled with an appropriate ideational content. Ultimately, they arrive at the same teleological conclusions - that is, on the one hand, by thinking about what the ultimate purpose of rationalism is and, on the other hand, what the goal of ideas and social cultures truly can be.

For example, scholars attempting to connect realism and constructivism are right in suggesting to focus on the social aspects of power. "Lying at the heart of a realist perspective on human nature, even before power or fear, is the observation that human beings are a social species."[40]

> Combining realism with constructivism should not suddenly lead to the sort of moral skepticism that is inherent in liberalism. It should instead lead to moral perspective that demands that particularism and universalism be, somehow, simultaneously respected.[41]

I thus suggest to look beyond what the three major schools of thought conceive of as the ultimate ends of actors' pursuits on an international scale, namely, power, wealth, ideas, and norms, and focus on the question of space and space politics as a final destination of actors' pursuits, ideas, and social norms which could provide a foundation for a greater cohesion between realism and constructivism. A constructivist reliance on shared modes of thinking and thus acting is somewhat insufficient. In addition to that, rationality can always be looked at as a form of idealism grounded in utilitarian modes of thinking; i.e., a pursuit of materialistic goals.

In a similar vein, it presupposes a perception of reality by an agent followed by a proper reaction to it in line with self-interest, an appropriate ideational framework of an agent and corresponding to the external structure, which thereby produces a renewed social kind. It is through the process of interaction between the agent and the structure that new social relations are being forged. I believe Wendt's branding of neorealism and neoliberal institutionalism as purely and exclusively "materialistic" is ambiguous as there is nothing in such approaches which defies the existence of a significant ideational component behind any kind of rationalist phenomena. For example, Morghenthau explicitly connects rationality to certain moral precepts in that a "rational foreign policy is good foreign policy" and that "only a rational foreign policy minimizes risks and maximizes benefits and, hence, complies with both the moral precept of prudence and the political requirement of success."[42]

As a matter of fact, there is clearly some degree of inconsistency which can be observed with respect to the nature of the behavior of atomic actors and social units vis-à-vis the universal ethical precepts accepted by the polities more generally. That is to say, what is it that accounts for a pernicious nature of behavior of some agents and social units and a benign nature of acts of others? For example, different state actors and individuals have diverging positions with respect to such issues as "security versus human rights", specifically, in times of serious national crises which thereby produces wide

political contentions and societal cleavages. Thus, there are shifting conceptions of "right and wrong" embraced by distinctive agents and groups that
come to power within a state and international system.

Realism finds an explanation to such processes in the "rational-egoistic
assumptions" and that some actors are driven by rationality to act in socially
"deleterious" ways while pursuing their objectives whereas some individuals
and social groups attain their goals in ways that can only be characterized as
socially "benevolent". Yet, what is it that accounts for such dramatic variations and perceptions of a "rationally-driven behavior" or conscience among
state actors? For instance, driven by what I would call particularistic perceptions of right and wrong, some agents tend to freely transgress the rights of
others and the general legal and ethical boundaries accepted by the state in
pursuing their ends whereas others do not act in such a way. Thus, there are
differential ways of interpreting and implementing a rational and moral element which explains a conflict of interest in different settings. In particular,
moral relativism addresses the problem of the multiplicity of the moral norm
among the distinctive regionally-defined communities.[43] Moreover, Velleman rightly suggests in this regard that "it is a moot question which one is
right" since a moral framework that each particular group may espouse is a
primary matter of concern on which all its political and ideological ideals are
ultimately being built and which juxtaposes communities one against the
other.[44] Along the lines of the social constructivism's conceptualization of
the social aspects of patterned behavior between actors, Velleman notes that:

> . . . members of a community construct a shared taxonomy of actions because
> they need to make sense of one another and to one another for the sake of
> social interaction. The social construction of action-types results in differences
> that stand in the way of moral disagreement between communities.[45]

He further elaborates on how moral norms come into existence:

> Because ordinariness is socially constructed, it is also local, in the sense that it
> is relative to some population of agents who interact regularly, usually because
> they live in one another's vicinity.[46]

However, I don't believe norms are necessarily socially constructed since
they are a product of ideas, whereas social norms are based on a shared
understanding of common good which can be considered as inherent rather
than socially acquired. Thus, social patterns are always a product of inherent
qualities of agents.

As a matter of fact, it points to distinctive and existentially sound interpretations of a rational element and rational acting by various state actors in
different settings. It likewise explains why various groups that come to power often tend to create new legal-rational systems of reference or adapt an old

one, specifically, in order to fit them to their indigenous moral concept and, thereby, inherently particularistic needs and interests. This is exemplified by the general practices among the newly formed governments to advance and adopt new policy initiatives related to most critical aspects of state politics, including defense, economy, foreign affairs, social welfare, and others in comparison to those of their predecessors.

Social constructivism addresses the question by what Wendt defines as "shared ideas and cultural bonds".[47] But since it can be claimed that deontological references are universal, how can one explain the divergent interpretation of and a compliance with what are commonly known as universal ethical precepts, particularly, when it comes to a prescriptive nature of universal rules and norms and differential compliance with those norms by particular state actors in different geo-political settings as well as the distinctive ontological explanations attached to a political identity? For example, the existence of the universal human rights convention to which most states are signatories highlights the situation of a formal compliance with universal ethical precepts pertaining to the respect of individual liberties and rights by both state and civil actors.

From its inception, the concept of human rights was grounded in a principle of universality. It is universality that makes human rights an inalienable part of modern civilization and a guarantor of freedom in all corners of the world. However, having accepted the universal nature of human rights, certain groups and particular polities strive to interpret them distinctively - that is, by adapting them to local rules and traditions and, thereby, rendering the universality principle futile since it mainly pertains to its universal relevance in each and all geopolitical settings. They thus create locally based interpretations and conceptualizations of human rights and thus human dignity, primarily attached to the dominating social group, or the group that holds the greatest amount of political power in any given polity.

The general problem of double standards and the duplication of a moral norm results from the divergent interpretations of what constitutes "decent behavior" and moral precepts among the distinctive agents and social groups alike which produces a general conflict and social factionalism. It likewise predominates an international political arena with dual standards responsible for most of today's major political contentiousness. For instance, for classical realists, violating the rights of others would be rationally sound in certain situations and even morally acceptable in order to reach a "rationally sound objective" such as the one which protects the will, integrity, prosperity, and interests of a group of individuals bound by common interests and inherent "links of allegiance". Social constructivists would in turn successfully explain that by conflicting ideas and social norms. However, neither school even attempts to account for the existence and centrality of double standards in producing wide political and social tensions. Ultimately, the indigenization of a moral element, the divergent interpretation and realization of a moral norm comes to serve as both a cause and a consequence of a protractible conflict among various communities. In addition to indigenization, the distinctive rationalizations of a moral element by communities pursuing various interests contribute to the aggravation of social hostility and serves as the basis of conflict.

According to Nye's framework of analysis, one can appeal to "a sense of attraction, love, or duty in our relationship and appeal to our shared values about the justness of contributing to those shared values and purposes."[48] Yet, Nye does not account for the highly selective nature of human behavior on which inter-state relations are built - that is, individuals cannot by their nature build long-lasting relationships randomly but only forge bonds based on their shared identities, which can be expressed in a myriad of ways, such as the political views, religious affiliation, ethnic, national and other relevant criteria. Therefore, the relations among nation states and the formation of coalitions depend in large part upon personal affiliations of state leaders and to what extent their backgrounds converge. Classical realists are right in emphasizing the inter-personal nature of international links but they do not account for the selective nature of human behavior in forging ties based on the inherent identity features.

> . . . communities can find themselves unable to disagree about what should be ordinarily done, because they disagree with respect to what is doable: there is no neutral domain of action-types from which they choose what to do. What is more, action-types are invented, and there is no domain of investable action-types from which communities can choose which ones to invent, much less disagree about such choices. Insofar as they can disagree about which action-types to invent, they disagree just by living differently, each converging on ordinary choices from among its own, socially constructed domain of doables.[49]
> Disagreement about morality is disagreement about what may or may not be done, and so it requires agreement about what is doable. For communities with different domains of doables, the question what may or may not be done is therefore moot.[50]

Unquestionably, states pursue self-interest, yet interests cannot be always perceived as being related to power as an end. Morghenthau asserts that a drive to dominate is the centerpiece of human relations. Classical realism views power as an end whereas neorealists believe it is security which states constantly seek to maximize. Rather, I believe that states often strive to maximize their power in relation to other states but power can likewise be seen as a means of advancing a greater goal, namely, space, and the homogeneity of social groups. There has not been afforded enough attention by scholars to the role of space as a primary aspect of state and foreign policies.

States seek to proliferate beyond their national boundaries but not in a conventional sense of expanding their nationhood or imposing their rule and hegemony on other states. I argue for a different interpretation of space and power politics which states seek to accomplish in an effort to achieve their goals which go beyond the conventional interpretations and understandings of statehood, power, self-interest, or welfare as ultimate ends in international politics. In that sense, states merely serve as a vehicle for competing identity groups which transcend the boundaries of modern nation states to materialize their goals related to the propagation across space and territorial dominance.

It would be more appropriate to presume how closely power, interest, and welfare relate to questions of space, territory, and the dynamics of space politics in the international political structure. As space is highly fractured so are the above mentioned forms of state politics since space is the ultimate objective of both the domestic policies and the international system. It is in the space that we must look for the interests of political actors at all levels of the structure, from domestic to international, as well as for the ontological and deontological content of state behavior in relations with other actors. The presumption that states seek to maximize their power ultimately raises a question what end that power ultimately aims to serve. Is the drive to dominate lies at the core of human nature? What really compels states to pursue dominance is a pursuit of spatial expansion. Why states or institutions which embody groups of states constantly vie for self-interest ranging from power, hegemony, economic welfare, or other ends? Realists and neorealists would explain that states maximize power in relation to other actors because hostility and a drive to dominate are inherent to human nature. Neorealists stress that a primary goal of states is security which leads them to adopt various patterns of behavior on an international level, from a military aggression to defensive politics, in relations with other states. They also argue that at the core of human nature lies self-interest embodied in egoism, rationality, aggression, and that makes the world system anarchical.

However, realists still firmly believe that states are connected to each other. Since state interests can be simultaneously at odds and intertwined owing to a communal structure of international order, how can one explain the nature of human society grounded in a general conflict of interest both among individuals and social groups? Interest, power, as well as the concentration of power by a number of agents manifests not only why but also how those agents confront each other and form alliances. That is to say, it is only against a certain group of actors that alliances are created since they must be looked at as the embodiment of a sum of interests and powers of individual actors bound by "links of allegiance", which can generally be defined in terms of a shared identity. It is these links that juxtapose individuals and social formations with other actors that bear a distinctive identity.

Relevant in this context is Walt's study which advances a theory of the "balance of threats", which he contrasts with Waltz's theory of the "balance of power" as well as a coinciding argument made by Morghethau.[51] In particular, Walt argues that states create alliances in order to "balance against threats".[52] He describes state motivations in entering alliances as "balancing" and "bandwagoning" vis-à-vis the adversary state, or the one that poses a certain amount of threat.[53]

Behind those interests there always lies power which defends them from other actors' interests. It is thus appropriate to conclude that according to this paradigm, concentration of power predetermines the nature of policies and ensures economic security among individual actors and groups of states bound by links of allegiance. No wonder that classical realism focuses primarily on a pursuit of power by state actors.

> The distribution of benefits is thus likely to reflect the distribution of power within an alliance, as is the determination of policies. A great power has a good chance to have its way with a weak ally as concerns benefits and policies.[54]

What neoliberals added to a neorealist conceptualization as to the nature of states' pursuits is that they create institutions in order to maximize their benefits and promote cooperation.

> . . . they [international regimes] are constructed principally by governments whose officials seek to further the interests of their states (as they interpret them) and of themselves. They seek wealth and power, and perhaps other values as well, no matter how much they may indulge in rhetoric about global welfare or a 'world safe for interdependence.'[55]

On the other hand, constructivists believe that shared ideas and interests are behind the social processes and allegiances which individuals and groups of actors create. Yet, these theories do not explain why actors always tend to forge alliances with certain actors against others as coalition-building always implies a concentration of military power and economic potential composed of the individual agents' contributions against another group of actors, whether agents or institutions, whose interests are seen as counterpoising. The nature of those alliances tends to change corresponding to the shifting ruling identity groups. Thus, states can join alliances and withdraw from them according to whether groups in power are aligned in terms of their identity group affiliation which produces both institutional cohesion and factionalism. Religiously and ideologically unaligned actors often collide on a political arena producing at times irreconcilable conflicts.

When state interests become infringed so do the interests of the perpetrators due to the interdependence inherent to the international society of states bound by common rules and norms, thereby initiating a retaliatory procedure incurred by the community. The latter is a view espoused by the English School and, in particular, Bull.[56] Thus, according to neorealism, the nature of the international system is, by and large, determined by the distribution of power as well as a deterrence factor between actors - that is, both states and institutions embodying groups of states, because of the security dilemma concerns prevalent among all its members. So, no matter how much military or economic power any given state possesses, it always has to abide by the rules accepted by the "community of states", which represent a majority of states bound by links of allegiance. But as Keohane asserts, the global political economy has been dominated by the American power and with its decline the role of transnational institutions and obligations inherent to such arrangements has eroded significantly which explains the opportunistic nature of policies which states increasingly seek to advance in relation to other states.

However, one needs to ask how the distribution of power occurs and what lies at the core of the power struggle process. On the other hand, power can be looked at as endogenously acquired, that is, as an objective of states in an anarchical global society. Since economic power is concomitant with the military preponderance, the world political system has always been characterized as being multipolar, rather than unipolar or bipolar, because of competing positions of polities all of which strive for the hegemonic status in relation to their competitors.

Realists clearly prefer a bipolar world system over a multipolar one as they believe it is more likely to be conducive to peace. However, a bipolar global order during the second half of the twentieth century has hardly proven to be a success in terms of preventing wars on a global scale during which time there occurred multiple conflicts between states and civil wars alike. Likewise, with the advent of globalization and the rise of transnational institutions there has been observed an increase in the number of internal conflicts. Thus, the view that a shift in a global order took place from the one type dominated by the two centers of political gravity to the one where a unipolar pattern of the distribution of power among polities prevails is ambiguous. Furthermore, even if we accept such a scenario, a change in a global polarity has not diminished the number of conflicts in the world. In particular, the nature of conflicts has not changed dramatically which undermines the argument made in favor of unipolarity which supposedly occurred after the Cold war between the Soviet Union and the United States ended, such as the one advanced by Fukuyama.[57] In addition, it undermines the main argument made by the democratic peace theory according to which with the advancement of liberal democratic regimes across the world the number of conflicts would diminish. All in all, the achievement of a homogeneous global political order is essentially impossible based on a permanent dualistic nature of all conflicts throughout the course of history.

As before, the vast majority of conflicts today can be described as bi-polar and dyadic, that is, civil wars, which always involve one party in power and another in the opposition. Both parties to any conflict have their respective constituencies among the general population as well as the links of allegiance with the external actors, whether states or identity groups. It is through those links that groups in power and opposition always seek to promote their influence vis-à-vis rival groups.

The world has always been characterized as having been dominated by sets of competing and contradicting ideas, as well as antagonistic social forces. A pursuit of hegemony and power per se cannot provide an explanation for the antagonisms among polities and various social transformations that are often taking place. Rather, their aspirations are driven by what neo-realists and neoliberals conceive as utilitarian pursuits which create competing social patterns among discreet polities as some states oftentimes cannot act cohesively with other states when it comes to co-working in alliances.

Neo-liberals would argue that states are driven by the rational-egoistic assumptions and a pursuit of economic power since it is in their best interests. States are impelled to cooperate, create transnational cooperative arrangements: e.g. regimes, in order to achieve a self-interest as well as common prosperity and thereby maintain peace. However, one simply cannot afford to describe state motivations in a process of forming and joining alliances as deriving exclusively from ego-centric assumptions or certain abstract common goals and pursuits. Rather, there are appropriate links of allegiance at play within institutions and alliances that can demonstrate a shared identity linkage among stakeholders seeking common goals, which, in turn, plays a salient role in the creation of alliances as well as in fostering factionalism among the distinctive agents within institutions.

> International regimes alter the information available to governments and the opportunities open to them; commitments made to support such institutions can only be broken at a cost to reputation. International regimes therefore change the calculations of advantage that governments make.[58]

According to neoliberals, international regimes foster cooperation even after hegemony, which initially sustained them, is gone.[59] It is owing to social interaction inherent to them that international regimes are sustained. Yet, war is not excluded even by neoliberals in certain situations as a factor in policy making in so far as it is intended to protect the economic interest or advance the economic preponderance of actors. "The sources of hegemony therefore include sufficient military power to deter or rebuff attempts to capture and close off important areas of the world political economy."[60] Keohane relies on "economic aspects of power, and on shifts in economic power as explanations for change." For neo-liberals, relying solely on military power to attain certain economic objectives is inefficient and futile, especially in the long run.

In contrast to the idealist conception and reliance on good motivations and a constructivist emphasis on the causality between ideas and structures, states are not so much concerned about the welfare of other states as they are about self-interest. Thus, rationalists essentially question the idealist and positivist conception of international peace as one based on a convergence of interest and a commonality of good motivations. From a realist perspective, motives of political actors are a negligible factor in a consideration of how to construct one's pattern of behavior vis-à-vis others. Realists are pessimistic about the role of motives as "[they] are the most illusive of psychological data, distorted as they are, frequently beyond recognition, by the interests and emotions of actor and observer alike"[61] In that respect, realists and neoliberals are in agreement as to the rational and utilitarian nature of political pursuits of actors. It is important for them that states make reciprocal adjustments to their behavior as a way to more effectively pursue their goals.

Both realists and neo-liberals maintain that states are bound by certain norms and regulations which constrain their conduct and thus avert a conflict, at least in theory. However weak they are in terms of enforcement, those norms and instruments are a cornerstone of modern global polity composed of sovereign actors. Wendt is critical of the neorealist conceptualization of patterned behavior as being based on shared norms and rules, rather than ideas.[62]

Analogous to the basic structure of human society where individuals possess a certain amount of freedom which is constrained from the moment a person comes to life as a member of the community and to the moment his life in a community ceases. Thus, freedom cannot be viewed as an absolute but only as a variable which is constrained by the mere fact that an individual, or a state, is not an atomic unit, but a social being, a member of the community of sovereign agents each of which possesses an equal amount of freedom and thus is endowed with an equal opportunity for self-realization as others. Realists are right in establishing a direct causal link between the amount of power and the amount of benefits, or space. Namely, a powerful state is likely to be more successful in attaining a greater amount of benefits, generally defined as space, than a less powerful state. It is exactly on this point that neoliberals try to complement a neorealist pursuit of power with appropriate transnational links which define actors' pursuits in terms of shared benefits and common purpose. Neorealists, such as Waltz and Walt, also argue that states temporarily create alliances even with adversaries in order to promote their own security, at least in a short run. Meanwhile, constructivists view political aspirations from the standpoint of shared ideas and identities.

Since freedom, both legalistic and physical, is a corollary of physical space, the freedom of individuals is constrained in that there exists a limited amount of physical space relative to a constantly growing population whose constituents tend to lay competing claims on space. With the increase in the number of agents significant constraints are being placed on private space. Ultimately, it is in the limitations of space that we must look for the constraints imposed on the private space and freedom by the public space which thereby generates conflicts among agents. In reality, however, realists argue that power is the decisive factor which determines the chance of both state survival and prosperity. Likewise, it is power that keeps the peace among nations and the balance of power makes states more prone to instigate conflicts. But in case of a community, freedom is not allegorical but in a literal sense individuals are confined to the private space which is endowed to them by the public space, a community of polities, and a majority of states, which is always embodied in certain formal and informal institutions of power.

Both neorealists and neoliberals heavily rely on a rationality of state behavior and "rational-egoistic assumptions" which states make in calculating their behavior toward other actors.[63] Keohane and Nye suggested an increased role of institutions which states created and accepted in order to bolster their ability to advance self-interest through the coordination of their policies.[64] John Ruggie brands the two approaches "neo-utilitarian" which depicts their shared perception of institutions in strictly instrumental terms. The two schools of thought differ on "the extent to which they believe institutions to play a significant role in international relations."[65] They "both [schools] explain patterns of interaction as the result of states, so conceived, using their capabilities to act on their preferences."[66] There are still differences between the major approaches in that "for neorealism the basic issues are survival and distributional conflict while for neoliberalism they involve the resolution of market failures."[67]

Hans Morghenthau asserts that "only a rational foreign policy minimizes risks and maximizes benefits and, hence, complies with both the moral precept of prudence and the political requirement of success."[68] From a realist perspective, this also accounts for the alliance-building and regime formation among state actors and various types of institutions, such as firms and corporations because of the overarching materialist pursuits of actors. However, viewing state behavior exclusively in light of the rationalism, pursuit of power and wealth is erroneous as it does not account for the overriding goal that states, and, for that matter, all other actors pursue throughout the course of their lifespan as state rationalism can only be ascribed to matters related to particularistic objectives of states related to self-survival, security, and prosperity. Classical realism stresses human nature and a drive for power to be the main components of global structure, while neorealism argues that states pursue security in an anarchical system.

Rather, states are ought to be looked at as an intermediary between actors and their goals. In other words, states must be viewed as a means of achieving the identity groups' aim related to the propagation across space. States must be looked at from a utilitarian perspective, or how they can be used by various competing groups to materialize their inherent objectives related to the proliferation across space. I thus suggest to look beyond a traditional national state paradigm, whether it be a minor state or a global power, in a global system, and focus on different groups that vie for dominance within and beyond the confines of polities in pursuing their inherent objectives. Those groups are primarily defined by their "links of allegiance" which transcend the political divides and whose constituents identify themselves by their belonging to a certain identity group defined in terms of ethnicity, nationality, race, religion, or other conventional aspects of group affiliation.

In a similar vein, states come to life constrained by their national boundaries by the nature of their existence in a finite space, as part of the community of nations. However, power is an ambiguous goal as is interest since both individuals and states do not seek to achieve power (both relative power imbalance and a balance of power), security, or wealth as an end in itself. I believe this is a major flaw of both neorealist and neoliberal approaches to international politics. Rather, power is a stepping stone to achieving a greater goal, namely, what agents and communities seek to attain in light of their natural desire to survive and prosper. What they ultimately seek is intimately tied to a drive to expand space-wise. Interest, derived from and embedded in interdependence, is what I would call a sign of a more serious concern which states have in relation to their self-survival pursuits and propagation across space. Thus, for instance, realists are right in that actors are bound to behave precisely in line with their calculations of the optimal behavior relative to other actors and in light of their indigenous moral-rational concept, what and how they envision their goals, paths of achieving them, and most efficient solutions to problems. Furthermore, they are only permitted to act in certain ways by way of the prevailing circumstances that they find themselves in and moral-rational frameworks they are driven by, which is in line with the English School's understanding of global society and, somewhat, with the constructivist views:

> ... states take into account the impact their decisions have on other members of their society. This is motivated in part by prudential considerations in so far as the survival of each community is dependent on the security of all. But there is more to the idea of international society. In addition to the fact of interdependence which generates common interests, states also have a capacity for sociality, manifested in the diffusion of shared values and in their general fidelity to the rules.[69]

[realism] requires indeed a sharp distinction between the desirable and the possible – between what is desirable everywhere and at all times and what is possible under the concrete circumstances of time and place. [70]

Aware of the evitable gap between good-, that is, rational - foreign policy and foreign policy as it actually is, political realism maintains not only that theory must focus upon rational elements of political reality but also that foreign policy ought to be rational in view of its own moral and practical purposes."[71]

I don't agree with a realist strict delineation between what they brand as "rational" and "other" frameworks on which agents, states, and institutions constantly rely in a process of interaction with other actors since actors are merely driven by some type of rational thinking which can have a discrepancy with other modes of rational thinking. That is to say, those variations can be seen to be in discord with respect to form and content but they represent essentially identical phenomena commonly defined as "rationally driven behavior". Thus, states and institutions are always driven by egoistic and utilitarian thinking in their pursuits of certain objectives but their modes of interpretation of what "objectivity" and "rationality" represents tend to be in discord which is expressed in their confronting political positions and general social contentiousness. However, I do not agree with Velleman's or, for that matter, the social constructivism's strictly geographical delineation of "relative moralities" and, thus, various forms of rationalism since they always tend to sustain close trans-regional ties with similar identity groups which builds into a global network of like-minded individuals and social groups firmly tied to space and bound by links of allegiance.

However, circumstances can also be seen to be the product of factors other than structural and systemic forces. For instance, much depends on how groups of states construct social patterns in relation to other actors, both states and institutions. The role of expectations has been emphasized by neoliberals and neorealists alike. So, each state can permit itself to act rationally, in ways that meet other actor's expectations and modes of thinking, in so far as that does not exceed certain constraints set forth by a broader community of polities. Once it acts irrationally, or contrary to the interests of the majority defined as the community and its particular members - that is, in ways that infringe on their rights and space, a set of informal rules comes into effect under the guise of the commonly accepted and enforceable norms, rules, instruments, and multiple enforcement institutions behind them. Thus, institutions are always formed and sustained by the will of the majority, which by far presents the most significant obstacles to their realization since a consensus within institutions is quite often inhibited by the prevailing contradictions among parties which form a majority as well as a minority which is always an integral part of the system ruled by the majority within the framework of overarching political agreements of which states and international institutions are one kind.

On the other hand, neorealists believe that at the core of the international system lies the process of distribution of power and the balancing of powers, as well as the corresponding changes in the military and resource capabilities which explains the instances of struggle for hegemony among states, especially among global powers. According to their explanation of international system, states are in a constant pursuit of the balance of power in relation to their adversaries, both real and potential. However, there exists a high degree of uncertainty about how the balance of power is interpreted by state actors. For instance, states constantly seek superiority, not hegemony, only in relations with their adversaries that simultaneously possess the capacity to transform into allies given a shift of the governments representing a distinctive political identity, which thereby undercuts the argument that international structure is anarchical. The pattern of international relations renders it highly predictable. However, much depends on whether an aligning identity group holds power in another state which produces cooperation and eliminates the possibility of conflict.

States constantly seek to minimize the risks of being dominated by other states by maximizing their military and economic potentials as well as by forging and joining only certain alliances and not others - namely, those where occurs an alignment of the identity group in favor of any given state. In a similar fashion, hegemonic states likewise seek to prevent the rise of challengers to their power on an international scale. It thus becomes clear that all states differ in their military and economic potentials and only countries from the opposing groups of states tend to interact in adversarial ways. That is to say, there is a relative cohesion within blocs of states bound by links of allegiance. Therefore, this undercuts the main notion advanced by neorealists that international relations are driven by individualistic pursuits of security and the balance of powers by states as they are by their nature not strictly atomic agents within a system but are always tied to other nations by their shared interests and perceptions of common good, which is corroborated by the constructivist view of international affairs as primarily driven by the ideational aspects such as shared ideas, norms, cultures, and religion. Identity linkages among states are constantly being transformed, both weakened and consolidated, according to the changes that are taking place in the high echelons of power.

> . . . balance of power and policies aiming at its preservation are not only inevitable but are an essential stabilizing factor in a society of sovereign nations; and that the instability of the international balance of power is due not to the faultiness of the principle but to the particular conditions under which the principle must operate in a society of sovereign nations. [72]

Hans Morghenthau outlines the concept of equilibrium in international politics, which posits that:

> . . . the elements to be balanced are necessary for society or are entitled to exist and, second, that without a state of equilibrium among them one element will gain ascendency over the others, encroach upon their interests and rights, and may ultimately destroy them. [73]

That view has certain limitations in so far as it does not account for the nature and principal driving forces of state policies and thus alliance building initiatives, beyond those considered by classical realists, neorealists, and neoliberals such as utilitarianism, i.e., the balance of power, self-interest, and a pursuit of wealth. The nature of various alliances and the shifting patterns of behavior among states in regard to participation in certain security and cooperation blocs ultimately raise questions about the genuine motivations and pursuits of national states in those arrangements as states can likewise be seen as joining alliances for non-pragmatic considerations, such as those considered by social constructivists; i.e., shared ideas, state identities and their preferences. In addition, international regimes can be seen as the dynamic institutions where membership is not constant, but a variable which is determined by the existence of the appropriate inherent "links of allegiance" among the leaderships of stakeholder states. Changes in inter-state alliances produce transformations of state policies and even state identities, corresponding shifts of political elites and changing links of allegiance among the leadership of countries which envision distinctive ways of interaction with external actors, both states and institutions.

In Robert Keohane's view,

> regimes do not substitute for continuous calculations of self-interest (which are impossible), but rather provide rules of thumb to which other governments also adhere. These rules may provide opportunities for governments to bind their successors, as well as to make other governments' policies more predictable. [74]

Meanwhile, Morghethau claims that:

> A typical alliance attempts to transform a small fraction of the total interests of the contracting parties in to common policies and measures. Some of these interests are irrelevant to the purposes of the alliance, others support them, others diverge from them, and still others are incompatible with them. [75]

Although the English School has dubbed the international system as anarchical, it also provides it with a certain level of orderliness. In particular, according to the English School of thought, the international society of states is anarchical, albeit based on a system of common rules and norms, and is driven by state self-interest. Hedley Bull describes anarchy as absence of government or rule.[76] It is also believed to be driven by the balance of power which significantly contributes to the consolidation of freedom among actors. " . . . having established a systematic pattern of relations with one another, states then go on to constitute a society by making a collective commitment to observe certain shared norms, obey general rules and participate in common institutions."[77]

> States take into account the impact their decisions have on other members of their society. This is motivated in part by prudential considerations in so far as the survival of each community is dependent on the security of all.[78]
> The English school derived its core historical proposition about the normative structure of modern international society from Heeren: that it rests on a system of states the character of which is defined by the principle of internal freedom, established by agreements between states that reflect their common interest in mutual independence.[79]

Neorealists such as Kenneth Waltz and Stephen Van Evera argue that states have largely security concerns and thus pursue defensive and self-survival objectives in an anarchical global environment where power is the principal driver of struggle while Mearsheimer believes that states seek local hegemony through increasing their offensive potential, which results, among other things, in arms race and aggressive behavior of state actors. "The structure of the international system forces states which seek only to secure to act aggressively toward each other."[80] Mearsheimer's view is correct in that it explains the nature of why wars are oftentimes being waged by any one state on another state or groups of states.[81]

For example, Van Evera calls it a "first-move advantage" by which states can be propelled to launch a war of aggression on another state or groups of states.[82] On the other hand, states can launch a war on another state for reasons related to survival and out of defensive concerns, namely, in cases when there is an absence of explicit threats to state interest or to the survival of state regime, but in the presence of both domestic and external conditions conducive to the fall of the regime or to a possibility of its failure due to the interference by a third actor supporting a party in open confrontation with the government. Relevant in this context is what Van Evera suggests in terms of how relative power fluctuations ("windows of opportunity") can cause states to launch preventive attacks on other states.[83] "States adopt more expansionist foreign policies for both defensive and opportunistic reasons, when conquest is easy."[84]

In particular, he uses the case of the First World War as a platform to substantiate the offense-defense theory - namely, when states launch an offensive war as a means of self-defense. Along the lines of Van Evera's claim that "windows of opportunity" and "false optimism" can lead states to launch offensive wars, Mearsheimer likewise suggests that "because great powers are programmed for offense, an appeased state is likely to interpret any power concession by another state as a sign of weakness – as evidence that the appeaser is unwilling to defend the balance of power."[85]

However, from the standpoint of neoliberalism, which is at odds with both classical realism and neorealism in that respect, an act of appeasement would not necessarily mean a sign of weakness. It is more likely to be the sign of explicit concern on the part of an actor to confront new kinds of opportunities that may be offered to it by another party in order to alleviate tension and to resolve the conflict by means other than a military confrontation. Thus, a military aggression in the wake of a "false optimism" or perception of weakness would be premature and highly detrimental as history has shown in numerous cases. Thus, Mearsheimer's suggestion is somewhat dubious as is Van Evera's. Van Evera argues that states often tend to exaggerate "the size of windows of opportunity and vulnerability" and launch offensive wars because of such prevailing perceptions.[86]

The balance of power is something that states might be interested in pursuing because of the security dilemma concerns. From a realist perspective, the balance of power is an essential condition conducive to global peace which is attained through the individualistic pursuits of polities aimed at securing immunity from external threats, rather than definite structural forces at work within a world system whose aim is to distribute power among its most essential elements.

> . . . balance of power and policies aiming at its preservation are not only inevitable but are an essential stabilizing factor in a society of sovereign nations; and that the instability of the international balance of power is due not to the faultiness of the principle but to the particular conditions under which the principle must operate in a society of sovereign nations."[87]

However, the limited amounts of data available to the contenders, absence of trust in their motives, as well as rational concerns render the concept futile as states continuously seek dominance one over another. Wendt presents a plausible view as to what the process of political change in international politics represents. In particular, he defines structural change in international politics as "change from one culture of anarchy to another . . . . (from a Hobbesian state of enmity to the Lockean rivalry and down to Kantian friendship), rather than as a change in the distribution of material capabilities from a neorealist perspective."[88]

"Although a balance of power is more likely to produce deterrence than is imbalance of power, balanced power does not guarantee that deterrence will work."[89] This view lies at the core of his "offensive realism" approach. It is thus in the interests of states to seek a predominance in the military capabilities relative to other states. According to standard views, the global society of national states is in a constant state of anarchy in which hostility and suspicion among actors prevail. It is primarily driven by human struggle and instinct to dominate. An anarchical society of state polities is essentially devoid of the commonalities of interest and any viable supranational enforcement and regulation mechanisms due to the egoistic nature of actors' pursuits. Common interest is related to both common and individualistic pursuit of power and wealth, the reason why states create institutions in efforts to maximize the effectiveness of their attempts of gaining individual and common power as well as wealth. Yet, whether or not individuals have a vested interest in maximizing the individual and common power and wealth depends on their belonging to a certain identity group which is exemplified by their political, religious, ethnic, national, regional and other forms of identity expression.

The assumption that states constantly seek to achieve security owing to an anarchical global environment where no external actor can be trusted whatsoever is erroneous as there is a high degree of interdependence among certain communities situated in different localities due to their identity bonds. Peter Katzenstein is somewhat correct in arguing that it is all about "porous regions infused with American Imperium".[90] However, he does not unveil an essential element of global regionalization - that is, the connections among certain identity groups which transcend the national and regional divides and their struggle for dominance and power. This struggle can be characterized as state actors constantly striving to achieve superiority in the military and economic affairs relative to others across the political divides.

I believe the main deficiency of the approach espoused by neoliberals is in that they do not provide a substantive explanation of the causal factors behind the formation of institutions and regimes. Rather, Walt provides a more subtle explanation of coalition formation in light of the "balance of threats", rather than the balance of powers or a pursuit of wealth.[91] That is to say, states create institutions in order to forge a common interest and purpose as well as in order to juxtapose them with those of other actors, namely, groups of states. Thus, transnational institutions must only be looked at from a perspective of conflicting and contradictory interests among the communities of state actors.

It is owing to the absence of a sovereign, any form of supranational government, and cohesive coordination efforts that the global system is rendered anarchical. It is also due to the fact that most of today's states were created by former empires strictly in accordance with their geo-political interests and concerns as well as questions related to the geography of distribution of ethnic groups across the territory. It would be more appropriate to presume how shared interests can be the product of geo-spatial proximity among states since as a general practice states positioned in close proximity to one another perceive themselves to be allies in time of crises relative to those situated farther away, as demonstrated by the multiple regional partnerships and alliances as a result of the perceptions of collective vulnerability among them.

The English school, and in particular, Bull maintains that the interest pursued by states is tied to the interest of other members of an international society which thus produces a pattern of inter-dependence that is still embedded in an anarchical global system. It is anarchical in that no enforceable set of rules and bodies exists that could conform to certain standards the behavior of various state actors. However, over time practices produce norms, both formal and informal rules of behavior, and further result in the creation of transnational institutions. International institutions and numerous conventions adopted by all members of the global society of states embody those rules, yet the prevalence of factionalism still undermines their objectives and functions. States and particular governments always tend to selectively cooperate only with certain actors and not with others who are assessed on the basis of their closeness with respect to political identity, mutual trust, transparency, and thereby the prospects of higher returns from cooperation. In addition, the presence of competing interests among world powers make those institutions, mainly established by themselves, devoid of a significant value since some actors often tend to act in ways that contradict the universal prescriptive nature of international norms.

That is to say, some actors that come to power in countries can sometimes consciously violate the principles enshrined in international law and various conventions while others constantly abide by those norms. The same is true for individuals some of whom can often easily transgress the rights of others unlike those who always adhere to legal and moral precepts. Notwithstanding the educational level of individuals, all tend to act in accordance with the "indigenous" moral concept whereby certain groups are somehow predisposed to violate the rights of others.

States, both major and minor, can be seen to pursue utilitarian goals, often defined as wealth and power. More importantly, however, groups of states tend to act in ways that increase their shared returns relative to other groups of states. Factionalism in an international society of states is conducive to the formation of alliances among states and, more precisely, groups of states, which underlies the fact that power and wealth cannot be considered as a goal of states per se, but rather groups of states create alliances in order to increase their shared wealth and power in relation to other groups of actors and their interests which are viewed as being competitive. Thus, alliances are always created only vis-à-vis another alliance.

In a similar vein, a process of balance of powers must be looked at from a perspective of competing interests among groups of states, rather than atomic agents pursuing particularistic goals. Specifically, one group of global powers always seeks to ensure some degree of order among minor nations by way of their allied attempts to achieve a balance of power relative to another group of states. This reflects a bipolar world order, not one based not on a competition between two superpowers, but one in which two counterpoised groups of states or centers of political gravity constantly vie for dominance on a global scale. For example, notwithstanding the argumentations made in favor of the process of globalization and increasing economic interdependence among states, it conforms to the general state of rivalry in the relations between countries of the western and eastern civilization and their differential ways of mentality.

Constructivists underscore the role of "ideas" and "shared knowledge," "the character of international life is largely determined by the beliefs and expectations that states have about each other, and these are largely constituted by social rather than material structures."[92] Wendt argues that interests and preference are "socially constructed" rather than rationally driven. He asserts that "international structure consists fundamentally in shared knowledge."[93] Furthermore, Wendt suggests that the English School was a predecessor to modern constructivism in that it framed the international system as world society governed by shared norms and rules.[94] From the standpoint of constructivism, international relations are built primarily according to the social aspects of interaction among actors rather than in terms of what ends states pursue throughout the course of their existence. It is owing to this fact that they make a significant emphasis on an interaction between internal agents and external structures and how they produce different "social kinds" that social constructivists contribute to modern understanding of global structure.

> International relations, like all social relations, exhibit some degree of institutionalization: at minimum, a mutual intelligibility of behavior together with communicative mechanisms and organizational routines which make that possible.[95]

One could undoubtedly argue that focusing on state pursuits could provide at least some explanation of what constitutes the essence of international structure. However, one needs to pay an equal amount of attention to how state objectives are being approached by different elite groups that hold power in different political settings. More importantly, it is crucial to understand what factors play a central role in state actor's behavior vis-à-vis other actors, aside from conventional assessments generally made by political scholars. For instance, in some instances, notwithstanding the willingness and efforts, state regimes in various countries are simply unable to find a single point of convergence of interests in the bilateral relations and are thereby deprived of opportunities to pursue diplomatic ways of tackling issues.

For instance, individualists and holists (structuralists) differ in their approaches as to how international relations are constructed, namely, whether they are driven by the bottom-up interests or top-down structural-systemic forces.[96] "Whereas the latter aggregates upward from ontologically primitive agents, the former works downward from irreducible social structures."[97] In a similar vein, rationalists and constructivists diverge in their vision regarding the world system as to whether state identities and interests are driven by domestic or systemic factors.[98]

World systems theory is an example of a holistic approach to international affairs. World systems theory, whose main proponent is Wallerstein, stresses that the primary level of analysis in international relations is the world system, rather than a national state. At the core of the world systems paradigm is the division of labor among states, according to which states are divided into the core, semi-periphery, and peripheral and their respective roles in the global economy.[99]

I agree with Wendt in that "social kinds" are produced by both internal aspects (emphasized by a reductionist approach, i.e., the doctrine of atomism) and external structures (holism) and that viewing "social kinds" as existing independent of external structures is ambiguous.[100] It is thus erroneous to theorize about various domestic phenomena independent of systemic structures and developments which have a great effect on them. It is appropriate to assume that systemic processes not only influence but recreate and reproduce domestic structures.

Furthermore, most individualists treat identities and interests as exogenously given.[101] Individualists likewise focus on rationalism, which constitutes mainstream IR.[102]

> . . . what it [individualism] rules out is the possibility that social structures have constitutive effects on agents, since that would mean that structures cannot be reduced to the properties or interactions of ontologically primitive individuals.[103]

On the other hand, holists support such constitutive effects on agents. According to Wendt, there are multiple points of convergence between neorealism and neoliberalism on the one hand, and constructivism, on the other. In particular, the importance of state interests, the role of ideas, institutions, the possibility of progress, and prevalence of shared rules of behavior. However, there is also a significant degree of variation between those schools of thought, namely, ontological differences. Alexander Wendt is right in that neoliberalism merely "reduces itself to secondary status of cleaning up residual variance left unexplained by a primary theory."[104] Wendt is critical of neorealism in that it is not designed to explain the "identities" and "interests".[105]

He describes four causes of collective identity-formation: "interdependence, common fate, homogenization, and self-restraint."[106]

> . . . a rationalist model treats identities and interests as exogenously given and constant, and a constructivist model, drawing on symbolic interactionism, which treats them as endogenous and potentially changeable.[107]

Wendt defines structural change in international politics as "change from one culture of anarchy to another . . . . (from a Hobbesian state of enmity to Lockean rivalry and further to Kantian friendship, rather than as a change in the distribution of material capabilities from a neorealist perspective."[108]

> different cultures of anarchy are based on different kinds of roles in terms of which states represent Self and Other. I identify three roles, enemy, rival, and friend, and argue that they are constituted by, and constitute, three distinct, macro-level cultures of international politics, Hobbesian, Lockean, and Kantian respectively.[109]

We can observe such transformation taking place on the one hand, in the context of the globalization trends in which a nation-state still plays a central role, and, on the other, against the backdrop of the increasing role of the transnational financial system which erodes the classical definitions of a nation-state and state borders as delimiting the interest of states and populations to a particular geo-political space.

However, it does not fully describe itself as "transformation from one culture of anarchy to another" as behind those changes lie recurrent structural transformations which correspond to the shifting identity groups in power which constitute a socio-political milieu in any given polity, a process which I can characterize as being of a permanent nature. Much explanation of how the system is constituted can be found in the dynamics of how the distinctive social groups are represented in power and the patterns of rivalry among those groups on a political arena, what links sustain societal cohesion and community formation and how that is reflected in a process of power struggle taking place within polities. For instance, Peter Katzenstein points out a fluid nature of regions largely determined by the dynamic of internal processes.

> Regions are not simply physical constants or ideological constructs; they express changing human practices. Economic development, military expansion, and symbolic identification with particular places all can shift over time, and with them the boundaries and salient features of particular regions.[110]

As a social constructivist, Katzenstein focuses on a spatial dimension of international politics grounded in "porous regions deeply embedded in an American Imperium".[111] He believes that globalization and internationalization make regions porous and driven by dynamism.[112] He further suggests that only two of the worlds six power centers "lie outside of the American Imperium", namely, Russia and China. Katzenstein highlights two modes of power, a territorial and non-territorial, which empires project over space and peoples, such as those commonly associated with the imperial politics of the British Empire, the "American Imperium", the Habsburgh Empire, the Ottoman Empire, and the Soviet Empire, among others. "Imperium designates both formal and informal systems of rule, and a mixture of hierarchical and egalitarian political relations".[113]

> In its decisive victories over fascism in World War Two and over communism during cold war, the United States has demonstrated the entwining of its political, military, economic, and ideological powers, the foundations of its preeminence in world politics.[114]

However, he likewise distinguishes the "American Imperium" from other empires is that it stretches across the whole world, "has greater scope and greater depth".[115] "The relative importance of its territorial and nonterritorial power has waxed and waned, shaped by domestic political struggles between conflicting coalitions".[116]

Katzenstein defies John Mearsheimer's claim that the extent of imperial influence is limited by a finite nature of landmass, which is naturally confined by water, over which global powers constantly seek control. In differentiating between maritime empires (Thalassocracies) and land empires (Thellurocracies), Katzenstein draws particular attention to the global extent of American influence in a modern era.

> Regions have both material and symbolic dimensions, and we can trace them in patterns of behavioral interdependence and political practice. Regions reflect the power and purpose of states.[117]
>
> Regions are made porous by a variety of processes, vary greatly in their institutional forms, and differ in having (or not having) core states that support US power and purpose. The consequences of these regional factors for world order are extremely important in an era of US pre-eminence.[118]

While important in its own right, Peter Katzenstein's argument does not delve into how the process of regionalization truly comes about and what factors are most responsible for the dynamics of regional developments, the transformation of regions into pseudo-state structures, the dynamics of a power struggle within regional institutions, and the reasons why groups of states ultimately form coalitions, beyond the conventional interpretations of alliance building and regime-formation as a result of a pursuit of a common political and economic interest. While he recognizes the limited scope of American power, his major focus on "porous regions" somewhat advances modern understanding of "how the structure is constituted". That said, slight attention has been paid to the dynamics of interaction among various elite groups situated in different polities and occupying varying hierarchical strata which could shed light on the genuine motivations underlying various patterns of cooperation and hostility prevalent in international settings.

NOTES

1. Robert Keohane, *After Hegemony: Cooperation and Discord in the World Political Economy*, (Princeton Univ. Press), 1984.

2. Kenneth Waltz, *Man, the State, and War: A Theoretical Analysis*, (Columbia Univ. Press), 2001.

3. Alexander Wendt, *Social Theory of International Politics*, (Cambridge Univ. Press), 1999, p. 94.

4. Ibid., p. 93.

5. Ibid., p. 94.

6. Ibid.

7. Ibid., p. 94.

8. Ibid., p. 98.

9. Ibid.

10. Hans Morghenthau, Kenneth Thompson and David Clinton, *Politics among Nations: The Struggle for Power and Peace*, 7th edition, (McGraw-Hill Humanities/Social Sciences/ Languages), 2005.

11. Robert Keohane, *After Hegemony: Cooperation and Discord in the World Political Economy*, (Princeton Univ. Press), 1984, p. 20.

12. Ibid., p. 12.

13. Hans Morghenthau, Kenneth Thompson and David Clinton, *Politics among Nations: The Struggle for Power and Peace*, 7th edition, (McGraw-Hill Humanities/Social Sciences/ Languages), 2005.

14. See Joseph Nye, *Soft Power: the Means to Success in World Politics*, (Public Affairs), 2004, p. 5.

15. Ibid., p. 5.

16. Ibid.

17. Ibid., p. 6.

18. Ibid., p. 6.

19. John Ruggie, *Constructing the World Polity: Essays on International Institutionalization*, (Routledge), 1998, p. 9.

20. Stephen Walt, *The Origins of Alliance*, (Cornell Univ. Press), 1987.

21. Stephen Walt, "Alliance Formation and the Balance of World Powers," *International Security*, Vol. 9, Iss. 4, 1985, p. 4.

22. Emanuel Adler and Michael Barnett, *Security Communities*, (Cambridge Univ. Press), 1998.

23. Deutsch, Karl; et al., *Political Community and the North Atlantic Area: International Organization in the Light of Historical Experience*, (Princeton: Princeton University Press), 1957.

24. Ibid.

25. John Ruggie, *Constructing the World Polity: Essays on International Institutionalization*, (Routledge), 1998, p. 9.

26. Alexander Wendt, *Social Theory of International Politics*, (Cambridge Univ. Press), 1999, p. 43.

27. Ibid., p. 90.

28. Ibid., p. 31.

29. Ibid., p. 98.

30. Ibid., p. 57.

31. Ibid., p. 98.

32. Kenneth Waltz, *Man, the State, and War: A Theoretical Analysis*, (Columbia Univ. Press), 2001, p. 126.

33. Stephen Van Evera, *Causes of War, Power and the Roots of Conflict*, (Cornell Univ. Press), 1999.

34. Immanuel Wallerstein, *World Systems Analysis: An Introduction*, (Duke Univ. Press), 2004.

35. Alexander Wendt, *Social Theory of International Politics*, (Cambridge Univ. Press), 1999, p. 97.

36. Edward Hallet Carr, *The Twenty Years' Crisis, 1919-39: An Introduction to the Study of International Relations*, (New York: Perennial), 2001, pp. 208-223.

37. Alexander Wendt, *Social Theory of International Politics*, (Cambridge Univ. Press), 1999, p. 97.

38. Ibid., p. 57.

39. Hans Morghenthau, Kenneth Thompson and David Clinton, *Politics among Nations: The Struggle for Power and Peace*, 7th edition, (McGraw-Hill Humanities/Social Sciences/ Languages), 2005, p. 12.

40. Jennifer Sterling-Folker, "Realist Constructivism and Morality," The Forum, *International Studies Review*, 2004, (6), p. 342.

41. Ibid., p. 343.

42. Hans Morghenthau, Kenneth Thompson and David Clinton, *Politics among Nations: The Struggle for Power and Peace*, 7th edition, (McGraw-Hill Humanities/Social Sciences/ Languages), 2005, p. 12.

43. David Velleman, *Foundations for Moral Relativism*, (Open Book Publishers), 2013, p. 2.

44. Ibid., p. 2.

45. Ibid., p. 4.

46. Ibid., p. 24.

47. Alexander Wendt, *Social Theory of International Politics*, (Cambridge Univ. Press), 1999.

48. Joseph Nye, *Soft Power: The Means to Success in World Politics*, (Public Affairs), 2004, p. 7.

49. David Velleman, *Foundations for Moral Relativism*, (Open Book Publishers), 2013, p. 25.

50. Ibid., p. 25.

51. Walt, The Origins of Alliance: Alliance Formation and the Balance of World Power, *International Security*, Vol. 9, Iss. 4, 1985, pp. 3-43.

52. Ibid., p. 5.

53. Ibid.

54. Hans Morghenthau, Kenneth Thompson and David Clinton, *Politics among Nations: The Struggle for Power and Peace*, 7th edition, (McGraw-Hill Humanities/Social Sciences/ Languages), 2005, p. 196.

55. Robert Keohane, *After Hegemony: Cooperation and Discord in the World Political Economy*, (Princeton Univ. Press), 1984, p. 22.

56. Hedley Bull, *The Anarchical Society: A Study of Order in World Politics*, (Columbia Univ. Press), 1977.

57. Francis Fukuyama, *The End of History and the Last Man*, (Free Press), 2006.

58. Robert Keohane, *After Hegemony: Cooperation and Discord in the World Political Economy*, (Princeton Univ. Press), 1984, p. 26.

59. Ibid.

60. Ibid., p. 40.

61. Hans Morghenthau, Kenneth Thompson and David Clinton, *Politics among Nations: The Struggle for Power and Peace*, 7th edition, (McGraw-Hill Humanities/Social Sciences/ Languages), 2005, p. 5.

62. Alexander Wendt, *Social Theory of International Politics*, (Cambridge Univ. Press), 1999, p. 101.

63. Robert Keohane, *After Hegemony: Cooperation and Discord in the World Political Economy*, (Princeton Univ. Press), 1984.

64. Robert Keohane and Joseph Nye, "The End of the Cold War in Europe," in *After the Cold War: International Institutions and State Strategies in Europe, 1989-1991,*" eds. Keohane, R., Nye, J., Hoffman, S., (Cambridge: Harvard University Press), 1993, p. 2.

65. John Ruggie, *Constructing the World Polity: Essays on International Institutionalization*, (Routledge), 1998, p. 3.

66. Ibid., p. 9.

67. Krasner, Stephen; Haber, Stephen; Kennedy, David; "Brothers Under the Skin: Diplomatic History and International Relations," *International Security*, 22, 1997, p. 16.

68. Hans Morghenthau, Kenneth Thompson and David Clinton, *Politics among Nations: The Struggle for Power and Peace*, 7th edition, (McGraw-Hill Humanities/Social Sciences/ Languages), 2005, p. 12.

69. Tim Dunne, "Society and Hierarchy in International Relations," *International Relations*, Vol., 17, Iss., 3, 2003, p. 305.

70. Hans Morghenthau, Kenneth Thompson and David Clinton, *Politics among Nations: The Struggle for Power and Peace*, 7th edition, (McGraw-Hill Humanities/Social Sciences/ Languages), 2005, p. 6.

71. Ibid., p. 12.

72. Hans Morghenthau, Kenneth Thompson and David Clinton, *Politics among Nations: The Struggle for Power and Peace*, 7th edition, (McGraw-Hill Humanities/Social Sciences/ Languages), 2005, p. 179.

73. Ibid.

74. Robert Keohane, *After Hegemony: Cooperation and Discord in the World Political Economy*, (Princeton Univ. Press), 1984, p. 13.

75. Hans Morghenthau, Kenneth Thompson and David Clinton, *Politics among Nations: The Struggle for Power and Peace*, 7th edition, (McGraw-Hill Humanities/Social Sciences/ Languages), 2005, p. 195.

76. Hedley Bull, *The Anarchical Society: A Study of Order in World Politics*, (Columbia Univ. Press), 1977, p. 46

77. Keene, p. 13.

78. Tim Dunne, Society and Hierarchy in International Relations, *International Relations*, Vol., 17, Iss., 3, 2003, p. 305.

79. Keene, p. 22.

80. John Mearsheimer, *The Tragedy of Great Power Politics*, (W.W. Norton & Company), 2001.

81. Ibid.

82. Stephen Van Evera, *Causes of War, Power and the Roots of Conflict*, (Cornell Univ. Press), 1999, p. 5.

83. Ibid.

84. Ibid.

85. John Mearsheimer, *The Tragedy of Great Power Politics*, (W.W. Norton & Company), 2001.

86. Stephen Van Evera, *Causes of War, Power and the Roots of Conflict*, (Cornell Univ. Press), 1999, p. 6.

87. Hans Morghenthau, Kenneth Thompson and David Clinton, *Politics among nations: the struggle for power and peace*, 7th edition, (McGraw-Hill Humanities/Social Sciences/Languages), 2005, p. 179.

88. Alexander Wendt, *Social Theory of International Politics*, (Cambridge Univ. Press), 1999, p. 44.

89. John Mearsheimer, *The Tragedy of Great Power Politics*, (W.W. Norton & Company), 2001.

90. Peter Katzenstein, *A World of Regions: Asia and Europe in the American Imperium*, (Cornell Univ. Press), 2005.

91. Stephen Walt, *The Origins of Alliance*, (Cornell Univ. Press), 1987.

92. Alexander Wendt, *Social Theory of International Politics*, (Cambridge Univ. Press), 1999, p. 20.

93. Ibid., p. 31.

94. Ibid., p. 31.

95. John Ruggie, *Constructing the World Polity: Essays on International Institutionalization*, (Routledge), 1998, p. 2.

96. Alexander Wendt, *Social Theory of International Politics*, (Cambridge Univ. Press), 1999, p. 26.

97. Ibid., p. 26.

98. Ibid., p. 37.

99. Immanuel Wallerstein, *World Systems Analysis: An Introduction*, (Duke Univ. Press), 2004.

100. Alexander Wendt, *Social Theory of International Politics*, (Cambridge Univ. Press), 1999, p. 84.

101. Ibid., p. 27.

102. Ibid.

103. Ibid.

104. Ibid., p. 35.

105. Ibid.

106. Ibid., p. 44.

107. Ibid.

108. Ibid.

109. Ibid., p. 43.

110. Peter Katzenstein, *A World of Regions: Asia and Europe in the American Imperium*, (Cornell Univ. Press), 2005, p. 12.

111. Ibid., p. 1.

112. Ibid., p. 13.

113. Ibid., p. 5.

114. Ibid., p. 3.

115. Ibid., p. 5.

116. Ibid.

117. Ibid., p. 2.

118. Ibid., p. 13.